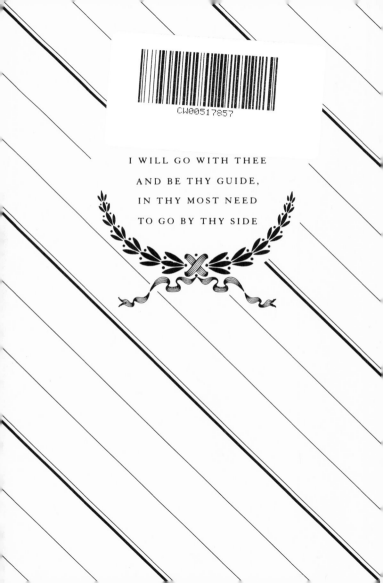

I WILL GO WITH THEE
AND BE THY GUIDE,
IN THY MOST NEED
TO GO BY THY SIDE

EVERYMAN'S LIBRARY
POCKET POETS

BYRON

····················

POEMS

EVERYMAN'S LIBRARY
POCKET POETS

This selection by Peter Washington first published in
Everyman's Library, 1994
© David Campbell Publishers Ltd., 1994

ISBN 1-85715-714-1

A CIP catalogue record for this book is available from the British Library

Published by David Campbell Publishers Ltd.,
79 Berwick Street, London W1V 3PF

Distributed by Random House (UK) Ltd.,
20 Vauxhall Bridge Road, London SW1V 2SA

Typography by Peter B. Willberg

Typeset by MS Filmsetting Ltd., Frome, Somerset

Printed and bound in Germany by
Mohndruck Graphische Betriebe GmbH, Gütersloh

CONTENTS

GEORGE GORDON
LORD BYRON

·················

POEMS

LYRIC VERSE

From HEBREW MELODIES
SHE WALKS IN BEAUTY

I

She walks in beauty, like the night
   Of cloudless climes and starry skies;
And all that's best of dark and bright
   Meet in her aspect and her eyes:
Thus mellow'd to that tender light
   Which heaven to gaudy day denies.

II

One shade the more, one ray the less,
   Had half impair'd the nameless grace
Which waves in every raven tress,
   Or softly lightens o'er her face;
Where thoughts serenely sweet express
   How pure, how dear their dwelling-place.

III

And on that cheek, and o'er that brow,
   So soft, so calm, yet eloquent,
The smiles that win, the tints that glow,
   But tell of days in goodness spent,
A mind at peace with all below,
   A heart whose love is innocent!

THE WILD GAZELLE

I

The wild gazelle on Judah's hills
    Exulting yet may bound,
And drink from all the living rills
    That gush on holy ground:
Its airy step and glorious eye
May glance in tameless transport by: —

II

A step as fleet, an eye more bright,
    Hath Judah witness'd there;
And o'er her scenes of lost delight
    Inhabitants more fair.
The cedars wave on Lebanon,
But Judah's statelier maids are gone!

III

More blest each palm that shades those plains
    Than Israel's scatter'd race;
For, taking root, it there remains
    In solitary grace:
It cannot quit its place of birth,
It will not live in other earth.

IV

But we must wander witheringly,
    In other lands to die;
And where our fathers' ashes be,
    Our own may never lie:
Our temple hath not left a stone,
And Mockery sits on Salem's throne.

OH! WEEP FOR THOSE

I

Oh! weep for those that wept by Babel's stream,
Whose shrines are desolate, whose land a dream;
Weep for the harp of Judah's broken shell;
Mourn – where their God hath dwelt the godless
    dwell!

II

And where shall Israel lave her bleeding feet?
And when shall Zion's songs again seem sweet?
And Judah's melody once more rejoice
The hearts that leap'd before its heavenly voice?

III

Tribes of the wandering foot and weary breast,
How shall ye flee away and be at rest!
The wild-dove hath her nest, the fox his cave,
Mankind their country – Israel but the grave!

MY SOUL IS DARK

I

My soul is dark – Oh! quickly string
    The harp I yet can brook to hear;
And let thy gentle fingers fling
    Its melting murmurs o'er mine ear.
If in this heart a hope be dear,
    That sound shall charm it forth again:
If in these eyes there lurk a tear,
    'Twill flow, and cease to burn my brain.

II

But bid the strain be wild and deep,
    Nor let thy notes of joy be first:
I tell thee, minstrel, I must weep,
    Or else this heavy heart will burst;
For it hath been by sorrow nursed,
    And ached in sleepless silence long;
And now 'tis doom'd to know the worst,
    And break at once – or yield to song.

VISION OF BELSHAZZAR

I

The King was on his throne,
    The Satraps throng'd the hall:
A thousand bright lamps shone
    O'er that high festival.
A thousand cups of gold,
    In Judah deem'd divine —
Jehovah's vessels hold
    The godless Heathen's wine!

II

In that same hour and hall,
    The fingers of a hand
Came forth against the wall,
    And wrote as if on sand:
The fingers of a man; —
    A solitary hand
Along the letters ran,
    And traced them like a wand.

III

The monarch saw, and shook,
    And bade no more rejoice;
All bloodless wax'd his look,
    And tremulous his voice.
'Let the men of lore appear,
    The wisest of the earth,
And expound the words of fear,
    Which mar our royal mirth.'

IV

Chaldea's seers are good,
    But here they have no skill;
And the unknown letters stood
    Untold and awful still.
And Babel's men of age
    Are wise and deep in lore;
But now they were not sage,
    They saw – but knew no more.

V

A captive in the land,
  A stranger and a youth,
He heard the king's command,
  He saw that writing's truth.
The lamps around were bright,
  The prophecy in view;
He read it on that night, —
  The morrow proved it true.

VI

'Belshazzar's grave is made,
  His kingdom pass'd away,
He, in the balance weigh'd,
  Is light and worthless clay;
The shroud his robe of state,
  His canopy the stone;
The Mede is at his gate!
  The Persian on his throne!'

THE DESTRUCTION OF SENNACHERIB

I

The Assyrian came down like the wolf on the fold,
And his cohorts were gleaming in purple and gold;
And the sheen of their spears was like stars on the sea,
When the blue wave rolls nightly on deep Galilee.

II

Like the leaves of the forest when Summer is green,
That host with their banners at sunset were seen:
Like the leaves of the forest when Autumn hath blown,
That host on the morrow lay wither'd and strown.

III

For the Angel of Death spread his wings on the blast,
And breathed in the face of the foe as he pass'd;
And the eyes of the sleepers wax'd deadly and chill,
And their hearts but once heaved, and for ever grew
    still!

IV

And there lay the steed with his nostril all wide,
But through it there roll'd not the breath of his pride;
And the foam of his gasping lay white on the turf,
And cold as the spray of the rock-beating surf.

V

And there lay the rider distorted and pale,
With the dew on his brow, and the rust on his mail:
And the tents were all silent, the banners alone,
The lances unlifted, the trumpet unblown.

VI

And the widows of Ashur are loud in their wail,
And the idols are broke in the temple of Baal;
And the might of the Gentile, unsmote by the sword,
Hath melted like snow in the glance of the Lord!

STANZAS FOR MUSIC

There be none of Beauty's daughters
   With a magic like thee;
And like music on the waters
   Is thy sweet voice to me:
When, as if its sound were causing
The charmed ocean's pausing,
The waves lie still and gleaming
And the lull'd winds seem dreaming:
And the midnight moon is weaving
   Her bright chain o'er the deep;
Whose breast is gently heaving,
   As an infant's asleep:
So the spirit bows before thee,
To listen and adore thee;
With a full but soft emotion,
Like the swell of Summer's ocean.

From HOURS OF IDLENESS
A FRAGMENT

When, to their airy hall, my father's voice
Shall call my spirit, joyful in their choice;
When, poised upon the gale, my form shall ride,
Or, dark in mist, descend the mountain's side;
Oh! may my shade behold no sculptured urns,
To mark the spot where earth to earth returns!
No lengthen'd scroll, no praise–encumber'd stone;
My epitaph shall be my name alone:
If *that* with honour fail to crown my clay,
Oh! may no other fame my deeds repay!
That, only *that*, shall single out the spot;
By that remember'd, or with that forgot.

                                                1803.

ON LEAVING NEWSTEAD ABBEY

'Why dost thou build the hall, son of the winged days?
Thou lookest from thy tower to-day: yet a few years,
and the blast of the desert comes, it howls in thy empty
court.' – OSSIAN.

Through thy battlements, Newstead, the hollow winds
    whistle;
  Thou, the hall of my fathers, art gone to decay;
In thy once smiling garden, the hemlock and thistle
  Have choked up the rose which late bloom'd in the
    way.

Of the mail-cover'd Barons, who proudly to battle
  Led their vassals from Europe to Palestine's plain,
The escutcheon and shield, which with every blast
    rattle,
  Are the only sad vestiges now that remain.

No more doth old Robert, with harp-stringing
    numbers,
  Raise a flame in the breast for the war-laurell'd
    wreath;
Near Askalon's towers, John of Horistan slumbers,
  Unnerved is the hand of his minstrel by death.

Paul and Hubert, too, sleep in the valley of Cressy;
   For the safety of Edward and England they fell:
My fathers! the tears of your country redress ye;
   How you fought, how you died, still her annals can
      tell.

On Marston, with Rupert, 'gainst traitors contending,
   Four brothers enrich'd with their blood the bleak
      field;
For the rights of a monarch their country defending,
   Till death their attachment to royalty seal'd.

Shades of heroes, farewell! your descendant, departing
   From the seat of his ancestors, bids you adieu!
Abroad, or at home, your remembrance imparting
   New courage, he'll think upon glory and you.

Though a tear dim his eye at this sad separation,
   'Tis nature, not fear, that excites his regret;
Far distant he goes, with the same emulation,
   The fame of his fathers he ne'er can forget.

That fame, and that memory, still will he cherish;
   He vows that he ne'er will disgrace your renown:
Like you will he live, or like you will he perish;
   When decay'd, may he mingle his dust with your
      own!

1803

DAMÆTAS

In law an infant, and in years a boy,
In mind a slave to every vicious joy;
From every sense of shame and virtue wean'd;
In lies an adept, in deceit a fiend;
Versed in hypocrisy, while yet a child;
Fickle as wind, of inclinations wild;
Woman his dupe, his heedless friend a tool;
Old in the world, though scarcely broke from school;
Damætas ran through all the maze of sin,
And found the goal when others just begin:
Even still conflicting passions shake his soul,
And bid him drain the dregs of pleasure's bowl;
But, pall'd with vice, he breaks his former chain,
And what was once his bliss appears his bane.

OCCASIONAL PIECES
SO, WE'LL GO NO MORE A ROVING

I

So, we'll go no more a roving
   So late into the night,
Though the heart be still as loving,
   And the moon be still as bright.

II

For the sword outwears its sheath,
   And the soul wears out the breast,
And the heart must pause to breathe,
   And love itself have rest.

III

Though the night was made for loving,
   And the day returns too soon,
Yet we'll go no more a roving
   By the light of the moon.

1817

TO THOMAS MOORE

I

My boat is on the shore,
    And my bark is on the sea;
But, before I go, Tom Moore,
    Here's a double health to thee!

II

Here's a sigh to those who love me,
    And a smile to those who hate;
And, whatever sky's above me,
    Here's a heart for every fate.

III

Though the ocean roar around me,
    Yet it still shall bear me on;
Though a desert should surround me,
    It hath springs that may be won.

IV

Were't the last drop in the well,
  As I gasp'd upon the brink,
Ere my fainting spirit fell,
  'Tis to thee that I would drink.

V

With that water, as this wine,
  The libation I would pour
Should be – peace with thine and mine,
  And a health to thee, Tom Moore.

JULY 1817.

EPIGRAM ON MY WEDDING-DAY

TO PENELOPE

This day, of all our days, has done
 The worst for me and you:—
'Tis just *six* years since we were *one*,
 And *five* since we were *two*.

JANUARY 2, 1821.

ON MY THIRTY-THIRD BIRTHDAY

JANUARY 22, 1821

Through life's dull road, so dim and dirty,
I have dragg'd to three-and-thirty.
What have these years left to me?
Nothing – except thirty-three.

MARTIAL, LIB. I, EPIG. I

'Hic est, quem legis, ille, quem requiris,
Tota notus in orbe Martialis,' &c.

He unto whom thou art so partial,
Oh, reader! is the well-known Martial,
The Epigrammatist: while living,
Give him the fame thou wouldst be giving;
So shall he hear, and feel, and know it –
    Post obits rarely reach a poet.

JOHN KEATS

Who kill'd John Keats?
    'I,' says the Quarterly,
So savage and Tartarly;
    ' 'Twas one of my feats.'

Who shot the arrow?
    'The poet-priest Milman
(So ready to kill man),
    Or Southey, or Barrow.'

JULY 1821.

TO THE COUNTESS OF BLESSINGTON

You have ask'd for a verse: — the request
    In a rhymer 'twere strange to deny;
But my Hippocrene was but my breast,
    And my feelings (its fountain) are dry.

Were I now as I was, I had sung
    What Lawrence has painted so well;
But the strain would expire on my tongue,
    And the theme is too soft for my shell.

I am ashes where once I was fire,
    And the bard in my bosom is dead;
What I loved I now merely admire,
    And my heart is as grey as my head.

My life is not dated by years —
    There are moments which act as a plough;
And there is not a furrow appears
    But is deep in my soul as my brow.

Let the young and the brilliant aspire
    To sing what I gaze on in vain;
For sorrow has torn from my lyre
    The string which was worthy the strain.

ON FINDING A FAN

In one who felt as once he felt,
    This might, perhaps, have fann'd the flame;
But now his heart no more will melt,
    Because that heart is not the same.

As when the ebbing flames are low,
    The aid which once improved their light,
And bade them burn with fiercer glow,
    Now quenches all their blaze in night.

Thus has it been with passion's fires —
    As many a boy and girl remembers —
While every hope of love expires,
    Extinguish'd with the dying embers.

The *first*, though not a spark survive,
    Some careful hand may teach to burn;
The *last*, alas! can ne'er survive;
    No touch can bid its warmth return.

Or if it chance to wake again,
    Not always doom'd its heat to smother,
It sheds (so wayward fates ordain)
    Its former warmth around another.

                    1807. [First published, 1832.]

TO THYRZA

Without a stone to mark the spot,
  And say, what Truth might well have said,
By all, save one, perchance forgot,
  Ah! wherefore art thou lowly laid?

By many a shore and many a sea
  Divided, yet beloved in vain;
The past, the future fled to thee,
  To bid us meet — no — ne'er again!

Could this have been — a word, a look,
  That softly said, 'We part in peace,'
Had taught my bosom how to brook
  With fainter sighs, thy soul's release.

And didst thou not, since Death for thee
  Prepared a light and pangless dart,
Once long for him thou ne'er shalt see,
  Who held, and holds thee in his heart?

Oh! who like him had watch'd thee here?
  Or sadly mark'd thy glazing eye,
In that dread hour ere death appear,
  When silent sorrow fears to sigh,

Till all was past? But when no more
   'Twas thine to reck of human woe,
Affection's heart-drops, gushing o'er,
   Had flow'd as fast – as now they flow.

Shall they not flow, when many a day
   In these, to me, deserted towers,
Ere call'd but for a time away,
   Affection's mingling tears were ours?

Ours too the glance none saw beside;
   The smile none else might understand;
The whisper'd thought of hearts allied,
   The pressure of the thrilling hand;

The kiss, so guiltless and refined,
   That Love each warmer wish forbore;
Those eyes proclaim'd so pure a mind,
   Even Passion blush'd to plead for more.

The tone, that taught me to rejoice,
   When prone, unlike thee, to repine;
The song, celestial from thy voice,
   But sweet to me from none but thine;

The pledge we wore – I wear it still,
  But where is thine? – Ah! where art thou?
Oft have I borne the weight of ill,
  But never bent beneath till now!

Well hast thou left in life's best bloom
  The cup of woe for me to drain.
If rest alone be in the tomb,
  I would not wish thee here again.

But if in worlds more blest than this
  Thy virtues seek a fitter sphere,
Impart some portion of thy bliss,
  To wean me from mine anguish here.

Teach me – too early taught by thee!
  To bear, forgiving and forgiven:
On earth thy love was such to me;
  It fain would form my hope in heaven!

OCTOBER 11, 1811.

THE CHAIN I GAVE

FROM THE TURKISH

The chain I gave was fair to view,
  The lute I added sweet in sound;
The heart that offer'd both was true,
  And ill deserved the fate it found.

These gifts were charm'd by secret spell,
  Thy truth in absence to divine;
And they have done their duty well, –
  Alas! they could not teach thee thine.

That chain was firm in every link,
  But not to bear a stranger's touch;
That lute was sweet – till thou could'st think
  In other hands its notes were such.

Let him who from thy neck unbound
  The chain which shiver'd in his grasp,
Who saw that lute refuse to sound,
  Restring the chords, renew the clasp.

When thou wert changed, they alter'd too;
  The chain is broke, the music mute.
'Tis past – to them and thee adieu –
  False heart, frail chain, and silent lute.

36

LINES WRITTEN ON A BLANK LEAF OF 'THE PLEASURES OF MEMORY'

Absent or present, still to thee,
    My friend, what magic spells belong!
As all can tell, who share, like me,
    In turn thy converse and thy song.

But when the dreaded hour shall come
    By Friendship ever deem'd too nigh,
And 'Memory' o'er her Druid's tomb
    Shall weep that aught of thee can die,

How fondly will she then repay
    Thy homage offer'd at her shrine,
And blend, while ages roll away,
    Her name immortally with *thine!*

                                  APRIL 19, 1812.

ODE TO NAPOLEON BUONAPARTE

> 'Expende Annibalem: – quot libras in duce summo
> Invenies?' – JUVENAL, *Sat.* x.

> 'The Emperor Nepos was acknowledged by the Senate,
> by the Italians, and by the Provincials of Gaul; his
> moral virtues, and military talents, were loudly cele-
> brated; and those who derived any private benefit from
> his government announced in prophetic strains the
> restoration of public felicity. ... By this shameful
> abdication, he protracted his life a few years, in a very
> ambiguous state, between an Emperor and an Exile,
> till ——.' —GIBBON's *Decline and Fall,* vol. vi, p. 220.

I

'Tis done – but yesterday a King!
    And arm'd with Kings to strive –
And now thou art a nameless thing:
    So abject – yet alive!
Is this the man of thousand thrones,
Who strew'd our earth with hostile bones,
    And can he thus survive?
Since he, miscall'd the Morning Star,
Nor man nor fiend hath fallen so far.

II

Ill-minded man! why scourge thy kind
    Who bow'd so low the knee?
By gazing on thyself grown blind,
    Thou taught'st the rest to see.
With might unquestion'd, – power to save, –
Thine only gift hath been the grave
    To those that worshipp'd thee;
Nor till thy fall could mortals guess
Ambition's less than littleness!

III

Thanks for that lesson – It will teach
    To after-warriors more
Than high Philosophy can preach,
    And vainly preach'd before.
That spell upon the minds of men
Breaks never to unite again,
    That led them to adore
Those Pagod things of sabre sway
With fronts of brass, and feet of clay.

IV

The triumph and the vanity,
    The rapture of the strife –
The earthquake voice of Victory,
    To thee the breath of life;
The sword, the sceptre, and that sway
Which man seem'd made but to obey,
    Wherewith renown was rife—
All quell'd! – Dark Spirit! What must be
The madness of thy memory!

V

The Desolator desolate!
    The Victor overthrown!
The Arbiter of others' fate
    A Suppliant for his own!
Is it some yet imperial hope
That with such change can calmly cope?
    Or dread of death alone?
To die a prince – or live a slave –
Thy choice is most ignobly brave!

VI

He who of old would rend the oak,
   Dream'd not of the rebound:
Chain'd by the trunk he vainly broke –
   Alone – how look'd he round?
Thou, in the sternness of thy strength,
An equal deed hast done at length,
   And darker fate hast found:
He fell, the forest prowlers' prey;
But thou must eat thy heart away!

VII

The Roman, when his burning heart
   Was slaked with blood of Rome,
Threw down the dagger – dared depart,
   In savage grandeur, home –
He dared depart in utter scorn
Of men that such a yoke had borne,
   Yet left him such a doom!
His only glory was that hour
Of self-upheld abandon'd power.

VIII

The Spaniard, when the lust of sway
    Had lost its quickening spell,
Cast crowns for rosaries away,
    An empire for a cell;
A strict accountant of his beads,
A subtle disputant on creeds,
    His dotage trifled well:
Yet better had he neither known
A bigot's shrine, nor despot's throne.

IX

But thou — from thy reluctant hand
    The thunderbolt is wrung —
Too late thou leav'st the high command
    To which thy weakness clung;
All Evil Spirit as thou art,
It is enough to grieve the heart
    To see thine own unstrung;
To think that God's fair world hath been
The footstool of a thing so mean;

X

And Earth hath spilt her blood for him,
   Who thus can hoard his own!
And Monarchs bow'd the trembling limb,
   And thank'd him for a throne!
Fair Freedom! we may hold thee dear,
When thus thy mightiest foes their fear
   In humblest guise have shown.
Oh! ne'er may tyrant leave behind
A brighter name to lure mankind!

XI

Thine evil deeds are writ in gore,
   Nor written thus in vain —
Thy triumphs tell of fame no more,
   Or deepen every stain:
If thou hadst died as honour dies,
Some new Napoleon might arise,
   To shame the world again —
But who would soar the solar height,
To set in such a starless night?

XII

Weigh'd in the balance, hero dust
    Is vile as vulgar clay;
Thy scales, Mortality! are just
    To all that pass away:
But yet methought the living great
Some higher sparks should animate,
    To dazzle and dismay:
Nor deem'd Contempt could thus make mirth
Of these, the Conquerors of the earth.

XIII

And she, proud Austria's mournful flower,
    Thy still imperial bride;
How bears her breast the torturing hour?
    Still clings she to thy side?
Must she too bend, must she too share
Thy late repentance, long despair,
    Thou throneless Homicide?
If still she loves thee, hoard that gem, –
'Tis worth thy vanish'd diadem!

XIV

Then haste thee to thy sullen Isle,
   And gaze upon the sea;
That element may meet thy smile –
   It ne'er was ruled by thee!
Or trace with thine all idle hand
In loitering mood upon the sand
   That Earth is now as free!
That Corinth's pedagogue hath now
Transferr'd his by-word to thy brow.

XV

Thou Timour! in his captive's cage
   What thoughts will there be thine,
While brooding in thy prison'd rage?
   But one – 'The world *was* mine!'
Unless, like he of Babylon,
All sense is with thy sceptre gone,
   Life will not long confine
That spirit pour'd so widely forth –
So long obey'd – so little worth!

XVI

Or, like the thief of fire from heaven,
    Wilt thou withstand the shock?
And share with him, the unforgiven,
    His vulture and his rock!
Foredoom'd by God – by man accurst,
And that last act, though not thy worst,
    The very Fiend's arch mock;
He in his fall preserved his pride,
And, if a mortal, had as proudly died!

XVII

There was a day – there was an hour,
    While earth was Gaul's – Gaul thine –
When that immeasurable power
    Unsated to resign
Had been an act of purer fame
Than gathers round Marengo's name,
    And gilded thy decline,
Through the long twilight of all time,
Despite some passing clouds of crime.

XVIII

But thou forsooth must be a king,
    And don the purple vest,
As if that foolish robe could wring
    Remembrance from thy breast.
Where is that faded garment? where
The gewgaws thou wert fond to wear,
    The star, the string, the crest?
Vain froward child of empire! say,
Are all thy playthings snatched away?

XIX

Where may the wearied eye repose
    When gazing on the Great;
Where neither guilty glory glows,
    Nor despicable state?
Yes – one – the first – the last – the best –
The Cincinnatus of the West,
    Whom envy dared not hate,
Bequeath'd the name of Washington,
To make man blush there was but one!

A SKETCH

'Honest – honest Iago!
If that thou be'st a devil, I cannot kill thee.'
                                        SHAKESPEARE.

Born in the garret, in the kitchen bred,
Promoted thence to deck her mistress' head;
Next – for some gracious service unexpress'd,
And from its wages only to be guess'd –
Raised from the toilette to the table, – where
Her wondering betters wait behind her chair.
With eye unmoved, and forehead unabash'd,
She dines from off the plate she lately wash'd.
Quick with the tale, and ready with the lie,
The genial confidante, and general spy,
Who could, ye gods! her next employment guess –
An only infant's earliest governess!
She taught the child to read, and taught so well,
That she herself, by teaching, learn'd to spell.
An adept next in penmanship she grows,
As many a nameless slander deftly shows:
What she had made the pupil of her art,
None know – but that high Soul secured the heart,
And panted for the truth it could not hear,
With longing breast and undeluded ear.
Foil'd was perversion by that youthful mind,
Which Flattery fool'd not, Baseness could not blind,

48

Deceit infect not, near Contagion soil,
Indulgence weaken, nor Example spoil,
Nor master'd Science tempt her to look down
On humbler talents with a pitying frown,
Nor Genius swell, nor Beauty render vain,
Nor Envy ruffle to retaliate pain,
Nor Fortune change, Pride raise, nor Passion bow,
Nor virtue teach austerity – till now.
Serenely purest of her sex that live,
But wanting one sweet weakness – to forgive,
Too shock'd at faults her soul can never know,
She deems that all could be like her below:
Foe to all vice, yet hardly Virtue's friend,
For Virtue pardons those she would amend.

But to the theme, now laid aside too long,
The baleful burthen of this honest song,
Though all her former functions are no more,
She rules the circle which she served before.
If mothers – none know why – before her quake;
If daughters dread her for the mothers' sake;
If early habits – those false links, which bind
At times the loftiest to the meanest mind –
Have given her power too deeply to instil
The angry essence of her deadly will;
If like a snake she steal within your walls,
Till the black slime betray her as she crawls;
If like a viper to the heart she wind,

And leave the venom there she did not find;
What marvel that this hag of hatred works
Eternal evil latent as she lurks,
To make a Pandemonium where she dwells,
And reign the Hecate of domestic hells?
Skill'd by a touch to deepen scandal's tints
With all the kind mendacity of hints,
While mingling truth with falsehood, sneers with
     smiles,
A thread of candour with a web of wiles:
A plain blunt show of briefly-spoken seeming,
To hide her bloodless heart's soul-harden'd scheming;
A lip of lies; a face form'd to conceal,
And, without feeling, mock at all who feel:
With a vile mask the Gorgon would disown, –
A cheek of parchment, and an eye of stone.
Mark, how the channels of her yellow blood
Ooze to her skin, and stagnate there to mud,
Cased like the centipede in saffron mail,
Or darker greenness of the scorpion's scale –
(For drawn from reptiles only may we trace
Congenial colours in that soul or face) –
Look on her features! and behold her mind
As in a mirror of itself defined:
Look on the picture! deem it not o'ercharged –
There is no trait which might not be enlarged:
Yet true to 'Nature's journeymen,' who made

This monster when their mistress left off trade –
This female dog-star of her little sky,
Where all beneath her influence droop or die.

Oh! wretch without a tear – without a thought,
Save joy above the ruin thou hast wrought –
The time shall come, nor long remote, when thou
Shalt feel far more than thou inflictest now;
Feel for thy vile self-loving self in vain,
And turn thee howling in unpitied pain.
May the strong curse of crush'd affections light
Back on thy bosom with reflected blight!
And make thee in thy leprosy of mind
As loathsome to thyself as to mankind!
Till all thy self-thoughts curdle into hate,
Black – as thy will for others would create:
Till thy hard heart be calcined into dust,
And thy soul welter in its hideous crust.
Oh, may thy grave be sleepless as the bed,
The widow'd couch of fire, that thou hast spread!
Then, when thou fain wouldst weary Heaven with
           prayer,
Look on thine earthly victims – and despair!
Down to the dust! – and, as thou rott'st away,
Even worms shall perish on thy poisonous clay.
But for the love I bore, and still must bear,
To her thy malice from all ties would tear –

Thy name – thy human name – to every eye
The climax of all scorn should hang on high,
Exalted o'er thy less abhorr'd compeers—
And festering in the infamy of years.

MARCH 29, 1816.

THE DREAM

I

Our life is two-fold: Sleep hath its own world,
A boundary between the things misnamed
Death and existence: Sleep hath its own world,
And a wide realm of wild reality.
And dreams in their development have breath,
And tears, and tortures, and the touch of joy;
They leave a weight upon our waking thoughts,
They take a weight from off our waking toils,
They do divide our being; they become
A portion of ourselves as of our time,
And look like heralds of eternity;
They pass like spirits of the past, – they speak
Like Sibyls of the future: they have power –
The tyranny of pleasure and of pain;
They make us what we were not – what they will,
And shake us with the vision that's gone by,
The dread of vanish'd shadows – Are they so?
Is not the past all shadow? – What are they?
Creations of the mind? – The mind can make
Substance, and people planets of its own
With beings brighter than have been, and give
A breath to forms which can outlive all flesh.
I would recall a vision which I dream'd
Perchance in sleep – for in itself a thought,

A slumbering thought, is capable of years,
And curdles a long life into one hour.

II

I saw two beings in the hues of youth
Standing upon a hill, a gentle hill,
Green and of mild declivity, the last
As 'twere the cape of a long ridge of such,
Save that there was no sea to lave its base,
But a most living landscape, and the wave
Of woods and corn-fields, and the abodes of men
Scatter'd at intervals, and wreathing smoke
Arising from such rustic roofs; — the hill
Was crown'd with a peculiar diadem
Of trees, in circular array, so fix'd,
Not by the sport of nature, but of man:
These two, a maiden and a youth, were there
Gazing — the one on all that was beneath
Fair as herself — but the boy gazed on her;
And both were young, and one was beautiful:
And both were young — yet not alike in youth.
As the sweet moon on the horizon's verge,
The maid was on the eve of womanhood;
The boy had fewer summers, but his heart
Had far outgrown his years, and to his eye
There was but one beloved face on earth,
And that was shining on him: he had look'd

Upon it till it could not pass away;
He had no breath, no being, but in hers;
She was his voice; he did not speak to her,
But trembled on her words; she was his sight,
For his eye follow'd hers, and saw with hers,
Which colour'd all his objects: — he had ceased
To live within himself; she was his life,
The ocean to the river of his thoughts,
Which terminated all: upon a tone,
A touch of hers, his blood would ebb and flow,
And his cheek change tempestuously — his heart
Unknowing of its cause of agony.
But she in these fond feelings had no share:
Her sighs were not for him; to her he was
Even as a brother — but no more; 'twas much,
For brotherless she was, save in the name
Her infant friendship had bestow'd on him;
Herself the solitary scion left
Of a time-honour'd race. — It was a name
Which pleased him, and yet pleased him not — and
     why?
Time taught him a deep answer — when she loved
Another; even *now* she loved another,
And on the summit of that hill she stood
Looking afar if yet her lover's steed
Kept pace with her expectancy, and flew.

III

A change came o'er the spirit of my dream.
There was an ancient mansion, and before
Its walls there was a steed caparison'd;
Within an antique Oratory stood
The Boy of whom I spake; – he was alone,
And pale, and pacing to and fro: anon
He sate him down, and seized a pen, and traced
Words which I could not guess of; then he lean'd
His bow'd head on his hands, and shook as 'twere
With a convulsion – then arose again,
And with his teeth and quivering hands did tear
What he had written, but he shed no tears,
And he did calm himself, and fix his brow
Into a kind of quiet: as he paused,
The Lady of his love re-entered there;
She was serene and smiling then, and yet
She knew she was by him beloved, – she knew,
For quickly comes such knowledge, that his heart
Was darken'd with her shadow, and she saw
That he was wretched, but she saw not all.
He rose, and with a cold and gentle grasp
He took her hand; a moment o'er his face
A tablet of unutterable thoughts
Was traced, and then it faded, as it came;
He dropp'd the hand he held, and with slow steps
Retired, but not as bidding her adieu,

For they did part with mutual smiles; he pass'd
From out the massy gate of that old Hall,
And mounting on his steed he went his way;
And ne'er repass'd that hoary threshold more.

IV

A change came o'er the spirit of my dream.
The Boy was sprung to manhood: in the wilds
Of fiery climes he made himself a home,
And his soul drank their sunbeams: he was girt
With strange and dusky aspects; he was not
Himself like what he had been; on the sea
And on the shore he was a wanderer.
There was a mass of many images
Crowded like waves upon me, but he was
A part of all; and in the last he lay
Reposing from the noontide sultriness,
Couch'd among fallen columns, in the shade
Of ruin'd walls that had survived the names
Of those who rear'd them; by his sleeping side
Stood camels grazing, and some goodly steeds
Were fasten'd near a fountain; and a man
Clad in a flowing garb did watch the while,
While many of his tribe slumber'd around:
And they were canopied by the blue sky,
So cloudless, clear, and purely beautiful,
That God alone was to be seen in heaven.

V

A change came o'er the spirit of my dream.
The Lady of his love was wed with One
Who did not love her better: — in her home,
A thousand leagues from his, — her native home,
She dwelt, begirt with growing Infancy,
Daughters and sons of Beauty, — but behold!
Upon her face there was the tint of grief,
The settled shadow of an inward strife,
And an unquiet drooping of the eye,
As if its lid were charged with unshed tears.
What could her grief be? — she had all she loved,
And he who had so loved her was not there
To trouble with bad hopes, or evil wish,
Or ill-repress'd affliction, her pure thoughts.
What could her grief be? — she had loved him not,
Nor given him cause to deem himself beloved,
Nor could he be a part of that which prey'd
Upon her mind — a spectre of the past.

VI

A change came o'er the spirit of my dream.
The Wanderer was return'd. — I saw him stand
Before an Altar — with a gentle bride;
Her face was fair, but was not that which made
The Starlight of his Boyhood; — as he stood
Even at the altar, o'er his brow there came

58

The self-same aspect, and the quivering shock
That in the antique Oratory shook
His bosom in its solitude; and then –
As in that hour – a moment o'er his face
The tablet of unutterable thoughts
Was traced, – and then it faded as it came,
And he stood calm and quiet, and he spoke
The fitting vows, but heard not his own words,
And all things reel'd around him; he could see
Not that which was, nor that which should have been –
But the old mansion, and the accustom'd hall,
And the remember'd chambers, and the place,
The day, the hour, the sunshine, and the shade,
All things pertaining to that place and hour,
And her who was his destiny, – came back
And thrust themselves between him and the light:
What business had they there at such a time?

VII

A change came o'er the spirit of my dream.
The Lady of his love: – Oh! she was changed
As by the sickness of the soul; her mind
Had wander'd from its dwelling, and her eyes
They had not their own lustre, but the look
Which is not of the earth; she was become
The queen of a fantastic realm; her thoughts
Were combinations of disjointed things;

And forms impalpable and unperceived
Of others' sight familiar were to hers.
And this the world calls frenzy; but the wise
Have a far deeper madness, and the glance
Of melancholy is a fearful gift;
What is it but the telescope of truth?
Which strips the distance of its fantasies,
And brings life near in utter nakedness,
Making the cold reality too real!

VIII

A change came o'er the spirit of my dream.
The Wanderer was alone as heretofore,
The beings which surrounded him were gone,
Or were at war with him; he was a mark
For blight and desolation, compass'd round
With Hatred and Contention; Pain was mix'd
In all which was served up to him, until,
Like to the Pontic monarch of old days,
He fed on poisons, and they had no power,
But were a kind of nutriment; he lived
Through that which had been death to many men,
And made him friends of mountains: with the stars
And the quick Spirit of the Universe
He held his dialogues; and they did teach
To him the magic of their mysteries;
To him the book of Night was open'd wide,

And voices from the deep abyss reveal'd
A marvel and a secret – Be it so.

IX

My dream was past; it had no further change.
It was of a strange order, that the doom
Of these two creatures should be thus traced out
Almost like a reality – the one
To end in madness – both in misery.

JULY 1816.

EPISTLE TO MR. MURRAY

My dear Mr. Murray,
You're in a damn'd hurry,
 To set up this ultimate Canto;
But (if they don't rob us)
You'll see Mr. Hobhouse
 Will bring it safe in his portmanteau.

For the Journal you hint of,
As ready to print off,
 No doubt you do right to commend it;
But as yet I have writ off
The devil a bit of
 Our 'Beppo:' – when copied, I'll send it.

Then you've Sotheby's Tour, –
No great things, to be sure, –
 You could hardly begin with a less work;
For the pompous rascallion,
Who don't speak Italian
 Nor French, must have scribbled by guess work.

You can make any loss up
With 'Spence' and his gossip,
    A work which must surely succeed;
Then Queen Mary's Epistle-craft,
With the new 'Fytte' of 'Whistlecraft,'
    Must make people purchase and read.

Then you've General Gordon,
Who girded his sword on,
    To serve with a Muscovite master
And help him to polish
A nation so owlish,
    They thought shaving their beards a disaster.

For the man, 'poor and shrewd,'
With whom you'd conclude
    A compact without more delay,
Perhaps some such pen is
Still extant in Venice;
    But please, sir, to mention *your pay*.

VENICE, JANUARY 8, 1818.

FRAGMENT

On the back of the Poet's MS. of Don Juan Canto I.
I would to heaven that I were so much clay,
    As I am blood, bone, marrow, passion, feeling –
Because at least the past were pass'd away –
    And for the future – (but I write this reeling,
Having got drunk exceedingly to-day,
    So that I seem to stand upon the ceiling)
I say – the future is a serious matter –
And so – for God's sake – hock and soda-water!

NARRATIVE
VERSE

THE VISION OF JUDGMENT

I

Saint Peter sat by the celestial gate:
   His keys were rusty, and the lock was dull,
So little trouble had been given of late;
   Not that the place by any means was full,
But since the Gallic era 'eighty-eight'
   The devils had ta'en a longer, stronger pull,
And 'a pull altogether,' as they say
At sea – which drew most souls another way.

II

The angels all were singing out of tune,
   And hoarse with having little else to do,
Excepting to wind up the sun and moon,
   Or curb a runaway young star or two,
Or wild colt of a comet, which too soon
   Broke out of bounds o'er th' ethereal blue,
Splitting some planet with its playful tail,
As boats are sometimes by a wanton whale.

III

The guardian seraphs had retired on high,
    Finding their charges past all care below;
Terrestrial business fill'd nought in the sky
    Save the recording angel's black bureau;
Who found, indeed, the facts to multiply
    With such rapidity of vice and woe,
That he had stripp'd off both his wings in quills,
And yet was in arrear of human ills.

IV

His business so augmented of late years,
    That he was forced, against his will no doubt,
(Just like those cherubs, earthly ministers,)
    For some resource to turn himself about,
And claim the help of his celestial peers,
    To aid him ere he should be quite worn out
By the increased demand for his remarks:
Six angels and twelve saints were named his clerks.

V

This was a handsome board – at least for heaven;
    And yet they had even then enough to do,
So many conquerors' cars were daily driven,
    So many kingdoms fitted up anew;
Each day too slew its thousands six or seven,
    Till at the crowning carnage, Waterloo,
They threw their pens down in divine disgust –
The page was so besmear'd with blood and dust.

VI

This by the way; 'tis not mine to record
    What angels shrink from: even the very devil
On this occasion his own work abhorr'd,
    So surfeited with the infernal revel:
Though he himself had sharpen'd every sword,
    It almost quench'd his innate thirst of evil.
(Here Satan's sole good work deserves insertion –
'Tis, that he has both generals in reversion.)

VII

Let's skip a few short years of hollow peace,
  Which peopled earth no better, hell as wont,
And heaven none – they form the tyrant's lease,
  With nothing but new names subscribed upon't;
'Twill one day finish: meantime they increase,
  'With seven heads and ten horns,' and all in front,
Like Saint John's foretold beast; but ours are born
Less formidable in the head than horn.

VIII

In the first year of freedom's second dawn
  Died George the Third; although no tyrant, one
Who shielded tyrants, till each sense withdrawn
  Left him nor mental nor external sun:
A better farmer ne'er brush'd dew from lawn,
  A worse king never left a realm undone!
He died – but left his subjects still behind,
One half as mad – and t'other no less blind.

IX

He died! his death made no great stir on earth:
  His burial made some pomp; there was profusion
Of velvet, gilding, brass, and no great dearth
  Of aught but tears — save those shed by collusion.
For these things may be bought at their true worth;
  Of elegy there was the due infusion —
Bought also; and the torches, cloaks, and banners,
Heralds, and relics of old Gothic manners,

X

Form'd a sepulchral melodrame. Of all
  The fools who flock'd to swell or see the show,
Who cared about the corpse? The funeral
  Made the attraction, and the black the woe.
There throbb'd not there a thought which pierced the
      pall;
  And when the gorgeous coffin was laid low,
It seem'd the mockery of hell to fold
The rottenness of eighty years in gold.

XI

So mix his body with the dust! It might
 Return to what it *must* far sooner, were
The natural compound left alone to fight
 Its way back into earth, and fire, and air;
But the unnatural balsams merely blight
 What nature made him at his birth, as bare
As the mere million's base unmummied clay—
Yet all his spices but prolong decay.

XII

He's dead – and upper earth with him has done;
 He's buried; save the undertaker's bill,
Or lapidary scrawl, the world is gone
 For him, unless he left a German will:
But where's the proctor who will ask his son?
 In whom his qualities are reigning still,
Except that household virtue, most uncommon,
Of constancy to a bad, ugly woman.

XIII

'God save the king!' It is a large economy
    In God to save the like; but if he will
Be saving, all the better; for not one am I
    Of those who think damnation better still:
I hardly know too if not quite alone am I
    In this small hope of bettering future ill
By circumscribing, with some slight restriction,
The eternity of hell's hot jurisdiction.

XIV

I know this is unpopular; I know
    'Tis blasphemous; I know one may be damn'd
For hoping no one else may e'er be so;
    I know my catechism; I know we're cramm'd
With the best doctrines till we quite o'erflow;
    I know that all save England's church have
        shamm'd,
And that the other twice two hundred churches
And synagogues have made a *damn'd* bad purchase.

XV

God help us all! God help me too! I am,
    God knows, as helpless as the devil can wish,
And not a whit more difficult to damn,
    Than is to bring to land a late-hook'd fish,
Or to the butcher to purvey the lamb;
    Not that I'm fit for such a noble dish,
As one day will be that immortal fry
Of almost everybody born to die.

XVI

Saint Peter sat by the celestial gate,
    And nodded o'er his keys; when, lo! there came
A wondrous noise he had not heard of late —
    A rushing sound of wind, and stream, and flame;
In short, a roar of things extremely great,
    Which would have made aught save a saint exclaim;
But he, with first a start and then a wink,
Said, 'There's another star gone out, I think!'

XVII

But ere he could return to his repose,
    A cherub flapp'd his right wing o'er his eyes –
At which St. Peter yawn'd, and rubb'd his nose:
    'Saint porter,' said the angel, 'prithee rise!'
Waving a goodly wing, which glow'd, as glows
    An earthly peacock's tail, with heavenly dyes:
To which the saint replied, 'Well, what's the matter?
'Is Lucifer come back with all this clatter?'

XVIII

'No,' quoth the cherub; 'George the Third is dead.'
    'And who *is* George the Third?' replied the apostle:
'*What George? what Third?*' 'The king of England,' said
    The angel. 'Well! he won't find kings to jostle
Him on his way; but does he wear his head?
    Because the last we saw here had a tustle,
And ne'er would have got into heaven's good graces,
Had he not flung his head in all our faces.

XIX

'He was, if I remember, king of France;
    That head of his, which could not keep a crown
On earth, yet ventured in my face to advance
    A claim to those of martyrs – like my own:
If I had had my sword, as I had once
    When I cut ears off, I had cut him down;
But having but my *keys*, and not my brand,
I only knock'd his head from out his hand.

XX

'And then he set up such a headless howl,
    That all the saints came out and took him in;
And there he sits by St. Paul, cheek by jowl;
    That fellow Paul – the parvenù! The skin
Of St. Bartholomew, which makes his cowl
    In heaven, and upon earth redeem'd his sin,
So as to make a martyr, never sped
Better than did this weak and wooden head.

XXI

'But had it come up here upon its shoulders,
    There would have been a different tale to tell:
The fellow-feeling in the saint's beholders
    Seems to have acted on them like a spell,
And so this very foolish head heaven solders
    Back on its trunk: it may be very well,
And seems the custom here to overthrow
Whatever has been wisely done below.'

XXII

The angel answer'd, 'Peter! do not pout:
    The king who comes has head and all entire,
And never knew much what it was about —
    He did as doth the puppet — by its wire,
And will be judged like all the rest, no doubt:
    My business and your own is not to inquire
Into such matters, but to mind our cue —
Which is to act as we are bid to do.'

XXIII

While thus they spake, the angelic caravan,
    Arriving like a rush of mighty wind,
Cleaving the fields of space, as doth the swan
    Some silver stream (say Ganges, Nile, or Inde,
Or Thames, or Tweed), and 'midst them an old man
    With an old soul, and both extremely blind,
Halted before the gate, and in his shroud
Seated their fellow traveller on a cloud.

XXIV

But bringing up the rear of this bright host
    A Spirit of a different aspect waved
His wings, like thunder-clouds above some coast
    Whose barren beach with frequent wrecks is paved;
His brow was like the deep when tempest-toss'd;
    Fierce and unfathomable thoughts engraved
Eternal wrath on his immortal face,
And *where* he gazed a gloom pervaded space.

XXV

As he drew near, he gazed upon the gate
   Ne'er to be enter'd more by him or Sin,
With such a glance of supernatural hate,
   As made Saint Peter wish himself within;
He potter'd with his keys at a great rate,
   And sweated through his apostolic skin:
Of course his perspiration was but ichor,
Or some such other spiritual liquor.

XXVI

The very cherubs huddled all together,
   Like birds when soars the falcon; and they felt
A tingling to the tip of every feather,
   And form'd a circle like Orion's belt
Around their poor old charge; who scarce knew
      whither
   His guards had led him, though they gently dealt
With royal manes (for by many stories,
And true, we learn the angels all are Tories).

XXVII

As things were in this posture, the gate flew
    Asunder, and the flashing of its hinges
Flung over space an universal hue
    Of many-colour'd flame, until its tinges
Reach'd even our speck of earth, and made a new
    Aurora borealis spread its fringes
O'er the North Pole; the same seen, when ice-bound,
By Captain Parry's crew, in 'Melville's Sound.'

XXVIII

And from the gate thrown open issued beaming
    A beautiful and mighty Thing of Light,
Radiant with glory, like a banner streaming
    Victorious from some world-o'erthrowing fight:
My poor comparisons must needs be teeming
    With earthly likenesses, for here the night
Of clay obscures our best conceptions, saving
Johanna Southcote, or Bob Southey raving.

XXIX

'Twas the archangel Michael; all men know
   The make of angels and archangels, since
There's scarce a scribbler has not one to show,
   From the fiends' leader to the angels' prince;
There also are some altar-pieces, though
   I really can't say that they much evince
One's inner notions of immortal spirits;
But let the connoisseurs explain *their* merits.

XXX

Michael flew forth in glory and in good;
   A goodly work of him from whom all glory
And good arise; the portal past – he stood;
   Before him the young cherubs and saints hoary –
(I say *young*, begging to be understood
   By looks, not years; and should be very sorry
To state, they were not older than St. Peter,
But merely that they seem'd a little sweeter).

XXXI

The cherubs and the saints bow'd down before
   That arch-angelic hierarch, the first
Of essences angelical, who wore
   The aspect of a god; but this ne'er nursed
Pride in his heavenly bosom, in whose core
   No thought, save for his Master's service, durst
Intrude, however glorified and high;
He knew him but the viceroy of the sky.

XXXII

He and the sombre, silent Spirit met –
   They knew each other both for good and ill;
Such was their power, that neither could forget
   His former friend and future foe; but still
There was a high, immortal, proud regret
   In either's eye, as if 'twere less their will
Than destiny to make the eternal years
Their date of war, and their 'champ clos' the spheres.

XXXIII

But here they were in neutral space: we know
   From Job, that Satan hath the power to pay
A heavenly visit thrice a year or so;
   And that the 'sons of God', like those of clay,
Must keep him company; and we might show
   From the same book, in how polite a way
The dialogue is held between the Powers
Of Good and Evil – but 'twould take up hours.

XXXIV

And this is not a theologic tract,
   To prove with Hebrew and with Arabic,
If Job be allegory or a fact,
   But a true narrative; and thus I pick
From out the whole but such and such an act
   As sets aside the slightest thought of trick.
'Tis every tittle true, beyond suspicion,
And accurate as any other vision.

XXXV

The spirits were in neutral space, before
    The gate of heaven; like eastern thresholds is
The place where Death's grand cause is argued o'er,
    And souls despatch'd to that world or to this;
And therefore Michael and the other wore
    A civil aspect: though they did not kiss,
Yet still between his Darkness and his Brightness
There pass'd a mutual glance of great politeness.

XXXVI

The Archangel bow'd, not like a modern beau,
    But with a graceful Oriental bend,
Pressing one radiant arm just where below
    The heart in good men is supposed to tend;
He turn'd as to an equal, not too low,
    But kindly; Satan met his ancient friend
With more hauteur, as might an old Castilian
Poor noble meet a mushroom rich civilian.

XXXVII

He merely bent his diabolic brow
    An instant; and then raising it, he stood
In act to assert his right or wrong, and show
    Cause why King George by no means could or
        should
Make out a case to be exempt from woe
    Eternal, more than other kings, endued
With better sense and hearts, whom history mentions,
Who long have 'paved hell with their good intentions.'

XXXVIII

Michael began: 'What wouldst thou with this man,
    Now dead, and brought before the Lord? What ill
Hath he wrought since his mortal race began,
    That thou canst claim him? Speak! and do thy will,
If it be just: if in this earthly span
    He hath been greatly failing to fulfil
His duties as a king and mortal, say,
And he is thine; if not, let him have way.'

XXXIX

'Michael!' replied the Prince of Air, 'even here,
  Before the Gate of him thou servest, must
I claim my subject: and will make appear
  That as he was my worshipper in dust,
So shall he be in spirit, although dear
  To thee and thine, because nor wine nor lust
Were of his weaknesses; yet on the throne
He reign'd o'er millions to serve me alone.

XL

'Look to *our* earth, or rather *mine*; it was,
  Once, more thy master's: but I triumph not
In this poor planet's conquest; nor, alas!
  Need he thou servest envy me my lot:
With all the myriads of bright worlds which pass
  In worship round him, he may have forgot
Yon weak creation of such paltry things:
I think few worth damnation save their kings, –

XLI

'And these but as a kind of quit-rent, to
    Assert my right as lord: and even had
I such an inclination, 'twere (as you
    Well know) superfluous; they are grown so bad,
That hell has nothing better left to do
    Than leave them to themselves: so much more mad
And evil by their own internal curse,
Heaven cannot make them better, nor I worse.

XLII

'Look to the earth, I said, and say again:
    When this old, blind, mad, helpless, weak, poor
        worm
Began in youth's first bloom and flush to reign,
    The world and he both wore a different form,
And much of earth and all the watery plain
    Of ocean call'd him king: through many a storm
His isles had floated on the abyss of time;
For the rough virtues chose them for their clime.

XLIII

'He came to his sceptre young; he leaves it old:
  Look to the state in which he found his realm,
And left it; and his annals too behold,
  How to a minion first he gave the helm;
How grew upon his heart a thirst for gold,
  The beggar's vice, which can but overwhelm
The meanest hearts; and for the rest, but glance
Thine eye along America and France.

XLIV

"Tis true, he was a tool from first to last
  (I have the workmen safe); but as a tool
So let him be consumed. From out the past
  Of ages, since mankind have known the rule
Of monarchs – from the bloody rolls amass'd
  Of sin and slaughter – from the Cæsar's school,
Take the worst pupil; and produce a reign
More drench'd with gore, more cumber'd with the
    slain.

XLV

'He ever warr'd with freedom and the free:
  Nations as men, home subjects, foreign foes,
So that they utter'd the word "Liberty!"
  Found George the Third their first opponent.
    Whose
History was ever stain'd as his will be
  With national and individual woes?
I grant his household abstinence; I grant
His neutral virtues, which most monarchs want;

XLVI

'I know he was a constant consort; own
  He was a decent sire, and middling lord.
All this is much, and most upon a throne;
  As temperance, if at Apicius' board,
Is more than at an anchorite's supper shown.
  I grant him all the kindest can accord;
And this was well for him, but not for those
Millions who found him what oppression chose.

XLVII

'The New World shook him off; the Old yet groans
　　Beneath what he and his prepared, if not
Completed: he leaves heirs on many thrones
　　To all his vices, without what begot
Compassion for him – his tame virtues; drones
　　Who sleep, or despots who have now forgot
A lesson which shall be re-taught them, wake
Upon the thrones of earth; but let them quake!

XLVIII

'Five millions of the primitive, who hold
　　The faith which makes ye great on earth, implored
A *part* of that vast *all* they held of old, –
　　Freedom to worship – not alone your Lord,
Michael, but you, and you, Saint Peter! Cold
　　Must be your souls, if you have not abhorr'd
The foe to Catholic participation
In all the licence of a Christian nation.

XLIX

'True! he allow'd them to pray God; but as
    A consequence of prayer, refused the law
Which would have placed them upon the same base
    With those who did not hold the saints in awe.'
But here Saint Peter started from his place,
    And cried, 'You may the prisoner withdraw:
Ere heaven shall ope her portals to this Guelph,
While I am guard, may I be damn'd myself!

L

'Sooner will I with Cerberus exchange
    My office (and *his* is no sinecure)
Than see this royal Bedlam bigot range
    The azure fields of heaven, of that be sure!'
'Saint!' replied Satan, 'you do well to avenge
    The wrongs he made your satellites endure;
And if to this exchange you should be given,
I'll try to coax *our* Cerberus up to heaven!'

LI

Here Michael interposed: 'Good saint! and devil!
   Pray, not so fast; you both outrun discretion.
Saint Peter! you were wont to be more civil!
   Satan! excuse this warmth of his expression,
And condescension to the vulgar's level:
   Even saints sometimes forget themselves in session.
Have you got more to say?' – 'No.' – 'If you please,
I'll trouble you to call your witnesses.'

LII

Then Satan turn'd and waved his swarthy hand,
   Which stirr'd with its electric qualities
Clouds farther off than we can understand,
   Although we find him sometimes in our skies;
Infernal thunder shook both sea and land
   In all the planets, and hell's batteries
Let off the artillery, which Milton mentions
As one of Satan's most sublime inventions.

LIII

This was a signal unto such damn'd souls
    As have the privilege of their damnation
Extended far beyond the mere controls
    Of worlds past, present, or to come; no station
Is theirs particularly in the rolls
    Of hell assign'd; but where their inclination
Or business carries them in search of game,
They may range freely — being damn'd the same.

LIV

They're proud of this — as very well they may,
    It being a sort of knighthood, or gilt key
Stuck in their loins; or like to an 'entré'
    Up the back stairs, or such freemasonry.
I borrow my comparisons from clay,
    Being clay myself. Let not those spirits be
Offended with such base low likenesses;
We know their posts are nobler far than these.

LV

When the great signal ran from heaven to hell –
  About ten million times the distance reckon'd
From our sun to its earth, as we can tell
  How much time it takes up, even to a second,
For every ray that travels to dispel
  The fogs of London, through which, dimly beacon'd,
The weathercocks are gilt some thrice a year,
If that the *summer* is not too severe:

LVI

I say that I can tell – 'twas half a minute;
  I know the solar beams take up more time
Ere, pack'd up for their journey, they begin it;
  But then their telegraph is less sublime,
And if they ran a race, they would not win it
  'Gainst Satan's couriers bound for their own clime.
The sun takes up some years for every ray
To reach its goal – the devil not half a day.

LVII

Upon the verge of space, about the size
   Of half-a-crown, a little speck appear'd
(I've seen a something like it in the skies
   In the Ægean, ere a squall); it near'd,
And, growing bigger, took another guise;
   Like an aërial ship it tack'd, and steer'd,
Or *was* steer'd (I am doubtful of the grammar
Of the last phrase, which makes the stanza stammer; –

LVIII

But take your choice): and then it grew a cloud;
   And so it was – a cloud of witnesses.
But such a cloud! No land e'er saw a crowd
   Of locusts numerous as the heavens saw these;
They shadow'd with their myriads space; their loud
   And varied cries were like those of wild geese
(If nations may be liken'd to a goose),
And realised the phrase of 'hell broke loose.'

LIX

Here crash'd a sturdy oath of stout John Bull,
  Who damn'd away his eyes as heretofore:
There Paddy brogued 'By Jasus!' —
  'What's your wull?'
The temperate Scot exclaim'd: the French ghost swore
In certain terms I shan't translate in full,
  As the first coachman will; and 'midst the roar;
The voice of Jonathan was heard to express,
'*Our* president is going to war, I guess.'

LX

Besides there were the Spaniard, Dutch, and Dane;
  In short, an universal shoal of shades,
From Otaheite's isle to Salisbury Plain,
  Of all climes and professions, years and trades,
Ready to swear against the good king's reign,
  Bitter as clubs in cards are against spades:
All summon'd by this grand 'subpœna,' to
Try if kings mayn't be damn'd like me or you.

LXI

When Michael saw this host, he first grew pale,
  As angels can; next, like Italian twilight,
He turn'd all colours – as a peacock's tail,
  Or sunset streaming through a Gothic skylight
In some old abbey, or a trout not stale,
  Or distant lightning on the horizon *by* night,
Or a fresh rainbow, or a grand review
Of thirty regiments in red, green, and blue.

LXII

Then he address'd himself to Satan: 'Why –
  My good old friend, for such I deem you, though
Our different parties make us fight so shy,
  I ne'er mistake you for a *personal* foe;
Our difference is *political*, and I
  Trust that, whatever may occur below,
You know my great respect for you: and this
Makes me regret whate'er you do amiss –

LXIII

'Why, my dear Lucifer, would you abuse
   My call for witnesses? I did not mean
That you should half of earth and hell produce;
   'Tis even superfluous, since two honest, clean,
True testimonies are enough: we lose
   Our time, nay, our eternity, between
The accusation and defence: if we
Hear both, 'twill stretch our immortality.'

LXIV

Satan replied, 'To me the matter is
   Indifferent, in a personal point of view:
I can have fifty better souls than this
   With far less trouble than we have gone through
Already; and I merely argued his
   Late majesty of Britain's case with you
Upon a point of form: you may dispose
Of him; I've kings enough below, God knows!'

LXV

Thus spoke the Demon (late call'd 'multi-faced'
    By multo-scribbling Southey). 'Then we'll call
One or two persons of the myriads placed
    Around our congress, and dispense with all
The rest,' quoth Michael: 'Who may be so graced
    As to speak first? there's choice enough – who shall
It be?' Then Satan answer'd, 'There are many;
But you may choose Jack Wilkes as well as any.'

LXVI

A merry, cock-eyed, curious-looking sprite
    Upon the instant started from the throng,
Dress'd in a fashion now forgotten quite;
    For all the fashions of the flesh stick long
By people in the next world; where unite
    All the costumes since Adam's, right or wrong,
From Eve's fig-leaf down to the petticoat,
Almost as scanty, of days less remote.

LXVII

The spirit look'd around upon the crowds
    Assembled, and exclaim'd, 'My friends of all
The spheres, we shall catch cold amongst these clouds;
    So let's to business: why this general call?
If those are freeholders I see in shrouds,
    And 'tis for an election that they bawl,
Behold a candidate with unturn'd coat!
Saint Peter, may I count upon your vote?'

LXVIII

'Sir,' replied Michael, 'you mistake; these things
    Are of a former life, and what we do
Above is more august; to judge of kings
    Is the tribunal met: so now you know.'
'Then I presume those gentlemen with wings,'
    Said Wilkes, 'are cherubs; and that soul below
Looks much like George the Third, but to my mind
A good deal older – Bless me! is he blind?'

LXIX

'He is what you behold him, and his doom
    Depends upon his deeds,' the Angel said;
'If you have aught to arraign in him, the tomb
    Gives licence to the humblest beggar's head
To lift itself against the loftiest.' – 'Some,'
    Said Wilkes, 'don't wait to see them laid in lead,
For such a liberty – and I, for one,
Have told them what I thought beneath the sun.'

LXX

'*Above* the sun repeat, then, what thou hast
    To urge against him,' said the Archangel. 'Why,'
Replied the spirit, 'since old scores are past,
    Must I turn evidence? In faith, not I.
Besides, I beat him hollow at the last,
    With all his Lords and Commons: in the sky
I don't like ripping up old stories, since
His conduct was but natural in a prince.

LXXI

'Foolish, no doubt, and wicked, to oppress
    A poor unlucky devil without a shilling;
But then I blame the man himself much less
    Than Bute and Grafton, and shall be unwilling
To see him punish'd here for their excess,
    Since they were both damn'd long ago, and still in
Their place below: for me, I have forgiven,
And vote his "habeas corpus" into heaven.'

LXXII

'Wilkes,' said the Devil, 'I understand all this;
    You turn'd to half a courtier ere you died,
And seem to think it would not be amiss
    To grow a whole one on the other side
Of Charon's ferry; you forget that *his*
    Reign is concluded; whatso'er betide,
He won't be sovereign more: you've lost your labour,
For at the best he will but be your neighbour.

LXXIII

'However, I knew what to think of it,
    When I beheld you in your jesting way,
Flitting and whispering round about the spit
    Where Belial, upon duty for the day,
With Fox's lard was basting William Pitt,
    His pupil; I knew what to think, I say:
That fellow even in hell breeds farther ills;
I'll have him *gagg'd* – 'twas one of his own bills.

LXXIV

'Call Junius!' From the crowd a shadow stalk'd,
    And at the name there was a general squeeze,
So that the very ghosts no longer walk'd
    In comfort, at their own aërial ease,
But were all ramm'd, and jamm'd (but to be balk'd,
    As we shall see), and jostled hands and knees,
Like wind compress'd and pent within a bladder,
Or like a human colic, which is sadder.

LXXV

The shadow came – a tall, thin, grey-hair'd figure,
    That look'd as it had been a shade on earth;
Quick in its motions, with an air of vigour,
    But nought to mark its breeding or its birth;
Now it wax'd little, then again grew bigger,
    With now an air of gloom, or savage mirth;
But as you gazed upon its features, they
Changed every instant – to *what*, none could say.

LXXVI

The more intently the ghosts gazed, the less
    Could they distinguish whose the features were;
The Devil himself seem'd puzzled even to guess;
    They varied like a dream – now here, now there;
And several people swore from out the press,
    They knew him perfectly; and one could swear
He was his father: upon which another
Was sure he was his mother's cousin's brother:

LXXVII

Another, that he was a duke, or knight,
   An orator, a lawyer, or a priest,
A nabob, a man-midwife; but the wight
   Mysterious changed his countenance at least
As oft as they their minds; though in full sight
   He stood, the puzzle only was increased;
The man was a phantasmagoria in
Himself – he was so volatile and thin.

LXXVIII

The moment that you had pronounced him *one*,
   Presto! his face changed, and he was another;
And when that change was hardly well put on,
   It varied, till I don't think his own mother
(If that he had a mother) would her son
   Have known, he shifted so from one to t'other;
Till guessing from a pleasure grew a task,
At this epistolary 'Iron Mask.'

LXXIX

For sometimes he like Cerberus would seem –
   'Three gentlemen at once' (as sagely says
Good Mrs. Malaprop); then you might deem
   That he was not even *one*; now many rays
Were flashing round him; and now a thick steam
   Hid him from sight – like fogs on London days:
Now Burke, now Tooke, he grew to people's fancies,
And certes often like Sir Philip Francis.

LXXX

I've an hypothesis – 'tis quite my own;
   I never let it out till now, for fear
Of doing people harm about the throne,
   And injuring some minister or peer,
On whom the stigma might perhaps be blown;
   It is – my gentle public, lend thine ear!
'Tis that what Junius we are wont to call
Was *really*, *truly*, nobody at all.

LXXXI

I don't see wherefore letters should not be
    Written without hands, since we daily view
Them written without heads; and books, we see,
    Are fill'd as well without the latter too:
And really till we fix on somebody
    For certain sure to claim them as his due,
Their author, like the Niger's mouth, will bother
The world to say if *there* be mouth or author.

LXXII

'And who and what art thou?' the Archangel said.
    'For *that* you may consult my title-page,'
Replied this mighty shadow of a shade:
    'If I have kept my secret half an age,
I scarce shall tell it now.' – 'Canst thou upbraid,'
    Continued Michael, 'George Rex, or allege
Aught further?' Junius answer'd, 'You had better
First ask him for *his* answer to my letter:

LXXXIII

'My charges upon record will outlast
    The brass of both his epitaph and tomb.'
'Repent'st thou not,' said Michael, 'of some past
    Exaggeration? something which may doom
Thyself if false, as him if true? Thou wast
    Too bitter – is it not so? – in thy gloom
Of passion?' – 'Passion!' cried the phantom dim,
'I loved my country, and I hated him.

LXXXIV

'What I have written, I have written: let
    The rest be on his head or mine!' So spoke
Old 'Nominis Umbra'; and while speaking yet,
    Away he melted in celestial smoke.
Then Satan said to Michael, 'Don't forget
    To call George Washington, and John Horne Tooke,
And Franklin;' – but at this time there was heard
A cry for room, though not a phantom stirr'd.

LXXXV

At length with jostling, elbowing, and the aid
  Of cherubim appointed to that post,
The devil Asmodeus to the circle made
  His way, and look'd as if his journey cost
Some trouble. When his burden down he laid,
  'What's this?' cried Michael; 'why, 'tis not a ghost?'
'I know it,' quoth the incubus; 'but he
Shall be one, if you leave the affair to me.

LXXXVI

'Confound the renegado! I have sprain'd
  My left wing, he's so heavy; one would think
Some of his works about his neck were chain'd.
  But to the point; while hovering o'er the brink
Of Skiddaw (where as usual it still rain'd),
  I saw a taper, far below me, wink,
And stooping, caught this fellow at a libel —
No less on history than the Holy Bible.

LXXXVII

'The former is the devil's scripture, and
   The latter yours, good Michael: so the affair
Belongs to all of us, you understand.
   I snatch'd him up just as you see him there,
And brought him off for sentence out of hand:
   I've scarcely been ten minutes in the air –
At least a quarter it can hardly be:
I dare say that his wife is still at tea.'

LXXXVIII

Here Satan said, 'I know this man of old,
   And have expected him for some time here;
A sillier fellow you will scarce behold,
   Or more conceited in his petty sphere:
But surely it was not worth while to fold
   Such trash below your wing, Asmodeus dear:
We had the poor wretch safe (without being bored
With carriage) coming of his own accord.

LXXXIX

'But since he's here, let's see what he has done.'
   'Done!' cried Asmodeus, 'he anticipates
The very business you are now upon,
   And scribbles as if head clerk to the Fates.
Who knows to what his ribaldry may run,
   When such an ass as this, like Balaam's, prates?'
'Let's hear,' quoth Michael, 'what he has to say:
You know we're bound to that in every way.'

XC

Now the bard, glad to get an audience, which
   By no means often was his case below,
Began to cough, and hawk, and hem, and pitch
   His voice into that awful note of woe
To all unhappy hearers within reach
   Of poets when the tide of rhyme's in flow;
But stuck fast with his first hexameter,
Not one of all whose gouty feet would stir.

XCI

But ere the spavin'd dactyls could be spurr'd
    Into recitative, in great dismay
Both cherubim and seraphim were heard
    To murmur loudly through their long array;
And Michael rose ere he could get a word
    Of all his founder'd verses under way,
And cried, 'For God's sake stop, my friend! 'twere
        best –
Non Di, non homines – you know the rest.'

XCII

A general bustle spread throughout the throng,
    Which seem'd to hold all verse in detestation;
The angels had of course enough of song
    When upon service; and the generation
Of ghosts had heard too much in life, not long
    Before, to profit by a new occasion:
The monarch, mute till then, exclaim'd, 'What! what!
Pye come again? No more – no more of that!'

112

XCIII

The tumult grew; an universal cough
   Convulsed the skies, as during a debate,
When Castlereagh has been up long enough
   (Before he was first minister of state,
I mean – the *slaves hear now*); some cried 'Off, off!'
   As at a farce; till, grown quite desperate,
The bard Saint Peter pray'd to interpose
(Himself an author) only for his prose.

XCIV

The varlet was not an ill-favour'd knave;
   A good deal like a vulture in the face,
With a hook nose and a hawk's eye, which gave
   A smart and sharper-looking sort of grace
To his whole aspect, which, though rather grave,
   Was by no means so ugly as his case;
But that, indeed, was hopeless as can be,
Quite a poetic felony '*de se.*'

XCV

Then Michael blew his trump, and still'd the noise
    With one still greater, as is yet the mode
On earth besides; except some grumbling voice,
    Which now and then will make a slight inroad
Upon decorous silence, few will twice
    Lift up their lungs when fairly over-crow'd;
And now the bard could plead his own bad cause,
With all the attitudes of self-applause.

XCVI

He said – (I only give the heads) – he said,
    He meant no harm in scribbling; 'twas his way
Upon all topics; 'twas, besides, his bread,
    Of which he butter'd both sides; 'twould delay
Too long the assembly (he was pleased to dread),
    And take up rather more time than a day,
To name his works – he would but cite a few –
'Wat Tyler' – 'Rhymes on Blenheim' – 'Waterloo.'

XCVII

He had written praises of a regicide;
   He had written praises of all kings whatever;
He had written for republics far and wide,
   And then against them bitterer than ever;
For pantisocracy he once had cried
   Aloud, a scheme less moral than 'twas clever;
Then grew a hearty anti-jacobin –
Had turn'd his coat – and would have turn'd his skin.

XCVIII

He had sung against all battles, and again
   In their high praise and glory; he had call'd
Reviewing 'the ungentle craft,' and then
   Become as base a critic as e'er crawl'd –
Fed, paid, and pamper'd by the very men
   By whom his muse and morals had been maul'd:
He had written much blank verse, and blanker prose,
And more of both than anybody knows.

XCIX

He had written Wesley's life: – here turning round
    To Satan, 'Sir, I'm ready to write yours,
In two octavo volumes, nicely bound,
    With notes and preface, all that most allures
The pious purchaser; and there's no ground
    For fear, for I can choose my own reviewers:
So let me have the proper documents,
That I may add you to my other saints.'

C

Satan bow'd, and was silent. 'Well, if you,
    With amiable modesty, decline
My offer, what says Michael? There are few
    Whose memoirs could be render'd more divine.
Mine is a pen of all work; not so new
    As it was once, but I would make you shine
Like your own trumpet. By the way, my own
Has more of brass in it, and is as well blown.

CI

'But talking about trumpets, here's my Vision!
    Now you shall judge, all people; yes, you shall
Judge with my judgment, and by my decision
    Be guided who shall enter heaven or fall.
I settle all these things by intuition,
    Times present, past, to come, heaven, hell, and all,
Like King Alfonso. When I thus see double,
I save the Deity some worlds of trouble.'

CII

He ceased, and drew forth an MS.; and no
    Persuasion on the part of devils, saints,
Or angels, now could stop the torrent; so
    He read the first three lines of the contents;
But at the fourth, the whole spiritual show
    Had vanish'd, with variety of scents,
Ambrosial and sulphureous, as they sprang,
Like lightning, off from his 'melodious twang.'

CIII

Those grand heroics acted as a spell:
    The angels stopp'd their ears and plied their pinions;
The devils ran howling, deafen'd, down to hell;
    The ghosts fled, gibbering, for their own dominions –
(For 'tis not yet decided where they dwell,
    And I leave every man to his opinions);
Michael took refuge in his trump – but, lo!
His teeth were set on edge, he could not blow!

CIV

Saint Peter, who has hitherto been known
    For an impetuous saint, upraised his keys,
And at the fifth line knock'd the poet down;
    Who fell like Phaeton, but more at ease,
Into his lake, for there he did not drown;
    A different web being by the Destinies
Woven for the Laureate's final wreath, whene'er
Reform shall happen either here or there.

CV

He first sank to the bottom – like his works,
    But soon rose to the surface – like himself;
For all corrupted things are buoy'd like corks,
    By their own rottenness, light as an elf,
Or wisp that flits o'er a morass: he lurks,
    It may be, still, like dull books on a shelf,
In his own den, to scrawl some 'Life' or 'Vision,'
As Welborn says – 'the devil turn'd precisian.'

CVI

As for the rest, to come to the conclusion
    Of this true dream, the telescope is gone
Which kept my optics free from all delusion,
    And show'd me what I in my turn have shown;
All I saw farther, in the last confusion,
    Was, that King George slipp'd into heaven for one;
And when the tumult dwindled to a calm,
I left him practising the hundredth psalm.

From DON JUAN

'Difficile est propriè communia dicere.' – HORACE.

'Dost thou think, because thou art virtuous, there shall be no more cakes and ale? Yes, by Saint Anne, and ginger shall be hot i' the mouth, too!' – SHAKESPEARE, *Twelfth Night, or What You Will.*

CANTO THE FIRST

DEDICATION
I

Bob Southey! You're a poet – Poet-laureate,
    And representative of all the race;
Although 'tis true that you turn'd out a Tory at
    Last, – yours has lately been a common case;
And now, my Epic Renegade! what are ye at?
    With all the Lakers, in and out of place?
A nest of tuneful persons, to my eye
Like 'four and twenty Blackbirds in a pye;

II

'Which pye being open'd they began to sing'
    (This old song and new simile holds good),
'A dainty dish to set before the King,'
    Or Regent, who admires such kind of food; –
And Coleridge, too, has lately taken wing,
    But like a hawk encumber'd with his hood, –
Explaining metaphysics to the nation –
I wish he would explain his Explanation.

III

You, Bob! are rather insolent, you know,
    At being disappointed in your wish
To supersede all warblers here below,
    And be the only Blackbird in the dish;
And then you overstrain yourself, or so,
    And tumble downward like the flying fish
Gasping on deck, because you soar too high, Bob,
And fall, for lack of moisture quite a-dry, Bob!

IV

And Wordsworth, in a rather long 'Excursion'
   (I think the quarto holds five hundred pages),
Has given a sample from the vasty version
   Of his new system to perplex the sages;
'Tis poetry — at least by his assertion,
   And may appear so when the dog-star rages —
And he who understands it would be able
To add a story to the Tower of Babel.

V

You — Gentlemen! by dint of long seclusion
   From better company, have kept your own
At Keswick, and, through still continued fusion
   Of one another's minds, at last have grown
To deem as a most logical conclusion,
   That Poesy has wreaths for you alone:
There is a narrowness in such a notion,
Which makes me wish you'd change your lakes for
     ocean.

VI

I would not imitate the petty thought,
    Nor coin my self-love to so base a vice,
For all the glory your conversion brought,
    Since gold alone should not have been its price.
You have your salary: was't for that you wrought?
    And Wordsworth has his place in the Excise.
You're shabby fellows – true – but poets still,
And duly seated on the immortal hill.

VII

Your bays may hide the baldness of your brows –
    Perhaps some virtuous blushes; – let them go –
To you I envy neither fruit nor boughs –
    And for the fame you would engross below,
The field is universal, and allows
    Scope to all such as feel the inherent glow:
Scott, Rogers, Campbell, Moore, and Crabbe, will try
'Gainst you the question with posterity.

VIII

For me, who, wandering with pedestrian Muses,
  Contend not with you on the winged steed,
I wish your fate may yield ye, when she chooses,
  The fame you envy, and the skill you need;
And recollect a poet nothing loses
  In giving to his brethren their full meed
Of merit, and complaint of present days
Is not the certain path to future praise.

IX

He that reserves his laurels for posterity
  (Who does not often claim the bright reversion)
Has generally no great crop to spare it, he
  Being only injured by his own assertion;
And although here and there some glorious rarity
  Arise like Titan from the sea's immersion,
The major part of such appellants go
To – God knows where – for no one else can know.

X

If, fallen in evil days on evil tongues,
    Milton appealed to the Avenger, Time,
If Time, the Avenger, execrates his wrongs,
    And makes the word 'Miltonic' mean '*sublime*,'
He deign'd not to belie his soul in songs,
    Nor turn his very talent to a crime;
He did not loathe the Sire to laud the Son,
But closed the tyrant-hater he begun.

XI

Think'st thou, could he – the blind Old Man – arise,
    Like Samuel from the grave, to freeze once more
The blood of monarchs with his prophecies,
    Or be alive again – again all hoar
With time and trials, and those helpless eyes,
    And heartless daughters – worn – and pale – and
        poor;
Would *he* adore a sultan? *he* obey
The intellectual eunuch Castlereagh?

XII

Cold-blooded, smooth-faced, placid miscreant!
  Dabbling its sleek young hands in Erin's gore,
And thus for wider carnage taught to pant,
  Transferr'd to gorge upon a sister shore,
The vulgarest tool that Tyranny could want,
  With just enough of talent, and no more,
To lengthen fetters by another fix'd,
And offer poison long already mix'd.

XIII

An orator of such set trash of phrase
  Ineffably – legitimately vile,
That even its grossest flatterers dare not praise,
  Nor foes – all nations – condescend to smile;
Not even a sprightly blunder's spark can blaze
  From that Ixion grindstone's ceaseless toil,
That turns and turns to give the world a notion
Of endless torments and perpetual motion.

XIV

A bungler even in its disgusting trade,
    And botching, patching, leaving still behind
Something of which its masters are afraid,
    States to be curb'd, and thoughts to be confined,
Conspiracy or Congress to be made –
    Cobbling at manacles for all mankind –
A tinkering slave-maker, who mends old chains,
With God and man's abhorrence for its gains.

XV

If we may judge of matter by the mind,
    Emasculated to the marrow *It*
Hath but two objects, how to serve, and bind,
    Deeming the chain it wears even men may fit,
Eutropius of its many masters, – blind
    To worth as freedom, wisdom as to wit,
Fearless – because *no* feeling dwells in ice,
Its very courage stagnates to a vice.

XVI

Where shall I turn me not to *view* its bonds,
  For I will never *feel* them; – Italy!
Thy late reviving Roman soul desponds
  Beneath the lie this State-thing breathed o'er thee –
Thy clanking chain, and Erin's yet green wounds,
  Have voices – tongues to cry aloud for me.
Europe has slaves, allies, kings, armies still,
And Southey lives to sing them very ill.

XVII

Meantime, Sir Laureate, I proceed to dedicate,
  In honest simple verse, this song to you.
And, if in flattering strains I do not predicate,
  'Tis that I still retain my 'buff and blue;'
My politics as yet are all to educate:
  Apostasy's so fashionable, too,
To keep *one* creed's a task grown quite Herculean:
Is it not so, my Tory, ultra-Julian?

VENICE, *September 16*, 1818.

I

I want a hero: an uncommon want,
    When every year and month sends forth a new one,
Till, after cloying the gazettes with cant,
    The age discovers he is not the true one:
Of such as these I should not care to vaunt,
    I'll therefore take our ancient friend Don Juan —
We all have seen him, in the pantomime,
Sent to the devil somewhat ere his time.

II

Vernon, the butcher Cumberland, Wolfe, Hawke,
    Prince Ferdinand, Granby, Burgoyne, Keppel,
      Howe,
Evil and good, have had their tithe of talk,
    And fill'd their sign-posts then, like Wellesley now;
Each in their turn like Banquo's monarchs stalk,
    Followers of fame, 'nine farrow' of that sow:
France, too, had Buonaparté and Dumourier
Recorded in the Moniteur and Courier.

III

Barnave, Brissot, Condorcet, Mirabeau,
  Pétion, Clootz, Danton, Marat, La Fayette,
Were French, and famous people, as we know;
  And there were others, scarce forgotten yet,
Joubert, Hoche, Marceau, Lannes, Desaix, Moreau,
  With many of the military set,
Exceedingly remarkable at times,
But not at all adapted to my rhymes.

IV

Nelson was once Britannia's god of war,
  And still should be so, but the tide is turn'd;
There's no more to be said of Trafalgar,
  'Tis with our hero quietly inurn'd;
Because the army's grown more popular,
  At which the naval people are concern'd,
Besides, the prince is all for the land-service,
Forgetting Duncan, Nelson, Howe, and Jervis.

V

Brave men were living before Agamemnon
   And since, exceeding valorous and sage,
A good deal like him too, though quite the same none;
   But then they shone not on the poet's page,
And so have been forgotten: — I condemn none,
   But can't find any in the present age
Fit for my poem (that is, for my new one);
So, as I said, I'll take my friend Don Juan.

VI

Most epic poets plunge 'in medias res'
   (Horace makes this the heroic turnpike road),
And then your hero tells, whene'er you please,
   What went before — by way of episode,
While seated after dinner at his ease,
   Beside his mistress in some soft abode,
Palace, or garden, paradise, or cavern,
Which serves the happy couple for a tavern.

VII

That is the usual method, but not mine –
  My way is to begin with the beginning;
The regularity of my design
  Forbids all wandering as the worst of sinning,
And therefore I shall open with a line
  (Although it cost me half an hour in spinning)
Narrating somewhat of Don Juan's father,
And also of his mother, if you'd rather.

VIII

In Seville was he born, a pleasant city,
  Famous for oranges and women – he
Who has not seen it will be much to pity,
  So says the proverb – and I quite agree;
Of all the Spanish towns is none more pretty,
  Cadiz, perhaps – but that you soon may see: –
Don Juan's parents lived beside the river,
A noble stream, and call'd the Guadalquivir.

IX

His father's name was José – *Don*, of course,
   A true Hidalgo, free from every stain
Of Moor or Hebrew blood, he traced his source
   Through the most Gothic gentlemen of Spain;
A better cavalier ne'er mounted horse,
   Or, being mounted, e'er got down again,
Than José, who begot our hero, who
Begot – but that's to come——Well, to renew:

X

His mother was a learned lady, famed
   For every branch of every science known –
In every Christian language ever named,
   With virtues equall'd by her wit alone:
She made the cleverest people quite ashamed,
   And even the good with inward envy groan,
Finding themselves so very much exceeded
In their own way by all the things that she did.

XI

Her memory was a mine: she knew by heart
    All Calderon and greater part of Lopé,
So that if any actor miss'd his part
    She could have served him for the prompter's copy;
For her Feinagle's were an useless art,
    And he himself obliged to shut up shop – he
Could never make a memory so fine as
That which adorn'd the brain of Donna Inez.

XII

Her favourite science was the mathematical,
    Her noblest virtue was her magnanimity;
Her wit (she sometimes tried at wit) was Attic all,
    Her serious sayings darken'd to sublimity;
In short, in all things she was fairly what I call
    A prodigy – her morning dress was dimity,
Her evening silk, or, in the summer, muslin,
And other stuffs, with which I won't stay puzzling.

XIII

She knew the Latin – that is, 'the Lord's prayer,'
  And Greek – the alphabet – I'm nearly sure;
She read some French romances here and there,
  Although her mode of speaking was not pure;
For native Spanish she had no great care,
  At least her conversation was obscure;
Her thoughts were theorems, her words a problem,
As if she deem'd that mystery would ennoble 'em.

XIV

She liked the English and the Hebrew tongue,
  And said there was analogy between 'em;
She proved it somehow out of sacred song,
  But I must leave the proofs to those who've seen 'em,
But this I heard her say, and can't be wrong,
  And all may think which way their judgments lean
    'em,
    "Tis strange – the Hebrew noun which means "I
    am,"
The English always use to govern d – n.'

XV

Some women use their tongues – she *look'd* a lecture,
    Each eye a sermon, and her brow a homily,
An all-in-all sufficient self-director,
    Like the lamented late Sir Samuel Romilly,
The Law's expounder, and the State's corrector,
    Whose suicide was almost an anomaly –
One sad example more, that 'All is vanity,' –
(The jury brought their verdict in 'Insanity.')

XVI

In short, she was a walking calculation,
    Miss Edgeworth's novels stepping from their
        covers,
Or Mrs. Trimmer's books on education,
    Or 'Cœlebs' Wife' set out in quest of lovers,
Morality's prim personification,
    In which not Envy's self a flaw discovers;
To others' share let 'female errors fall,'
For she had not even one – the worst of all.

XVII

Oh! she was perfect past all parallel —
  Of any modern female saint's comparison;
So far above the cunning powers of hell,
  Her guardian angel had given up his garrison;
Even her minutest motions went as well
  As those of the best time-piece made by Harrison:
In virtues nothing earthly could surpass her,
Save thine 'incomparable oil,' Macassar!

XVIII

Perfect she was, but as perfection is
  Insipid in this naughty world of ours,
Where our first parents never learn'd to kiss
  Till they were exiled from their earlier bowers,
Where all was peace, and innocence, and bliss
  (I wonder how they got through the twelve hours),
Don José, like a lineal son of Eve,
Went plucking various fruit without her leave.

XIX

He was a mortal of the careless kind,
  With no great love for learning, or the learn'd,
Who chose to go where'er he had a mind,
  And never dream'd his lady was concern'd;
The world, as usual, wickedly inclined
  To see a kingdom or a house o'erturn'd,
Whisper'd he had a mistress, some said *two*,
But for domestic quarrels *one* will do.

XX

Now Donna Inez had, with all her merit,
  A great opinion of her own good qualities;
Neglect, indeed, requires a saint to bear it,
  And such, indeed, she was in her moralities;
But then she had a devil of a spirit,
  And sometimes mix'd up fancies with realities,
And let few opportunities escape
Of getting her liege lord into a scrape.

XXI

This was an easy matter with a man
    Oft in the wrong, and never on his guard;
And even the wisest, do the best they can,
    Have moments, hours, and days, so unprepared,
That you might 'brain them with their lady's fan';
    And sometimes ladies hit exceeding hard,
And fans turn into falchions in fair hands,
And why and wherefore no one understands.

XXII

'Tis pity learned virgins ever wed
    With persons of no sort of education,
Or gentlemen, who, though well born and bred,
    Grow tired of scientific conversation;
I don't choose to say much upon this head,
    I'm a plain man, and in a single station,
But – Oh! ye lords of ladies intellectual,
Inform us truly have they not hen-peck'd you all?

XXIII

Don José and his lady quarrell'd – *why*,
   Not any of the many could divine,
Though several thousand people chose to try,
   'Twas surely no concern of theirs nor mine;
I loathe that low vice – curiosity;
   But if there's anything in which I shine,
'Tis in arranging all my friends' affairs,
Not having, of my own, domestic cares.

XXIV

And so I interfered, and with the best
   Intentions, but their treatment was not kind;
I think the foolish people were possess'd,
   For neither of them could I ever find,
Although their porter afterwards confess'd –
   But that's no matter, and the worst's behind,
For little Juan o'er me threw, down stairs,
A pail of housemaid's water unawares.

XXV

A little curly-headed, good-for-nothing,
  And mischief-making monkey from his birth;
His parents ne'er agreed except in doting
  Upon the most unquiet imp on earth;
Instead of quarrelling, had they been but both in
  Their senses, they'd have sent young master forth
To school, or had him soundly whipp'd at home,
To teach him manners for the time to come.

XXVI

Don José and the Donna Inez led
  For some time an unhappy sort of life,
Wishing each other, not divorced, but dead;
  They lived respectably as man and wife,
Their conduct was exceedingly well-bred,
  And gave no outward signs of inward strife,
Until at length the smother'd fire broke out,
And put the business past all kind of doubt.

XXVII

For Inez call'd some druggists and physicians,
    And tried to prove her loving lord was *mad*,
But as he had some lucid intermissions,
    She next decided he was only *bad*;
Yet when they ask'd her for her depositions,
    No sort of explanation could be had,
Save that her duty both to man and God
Required this conduct – which seem'd very odd.

XXVIII

She kept a journal, where his faults were noted,
    And open'd certain trunks of books and letters,
All which might, if occasion served, be quoted;
    And then she had all Seville for abettors,
Besides her good old grandmother (who doted);
    The hearers of her case became repeaters,
Then advocates, inquisitors, and judges,
Some for amusement, others for old grudges.

XXIX

And then this best and meekest woman bore
   With such serenity her husband's woes,
Just as the Spartan ladies did of yore,
   Who saw their spouses kill'd, and nobly chose
Never to say a word about them more —
   Calmly she heard each calumny that rose,
And saw *his* agonies with such sublimity,
That all the world exclaim'd, 'What magnanimity!'

XXX

No doubt this patience, when the world is damning us,
   Is philosophic in our former friends;
'Tis also pleasant to be deem'd magnanimous,
   The more so in obtaining our own ends;
And what the lawyers call a '*malus animus*'
   Conduct like this by no means comprehends:
Revenge in person's certainly no virtue,
But then 'tis not *my* fault, if *others* hurt you.

XXXI

And if our quarrels should rip up old stories,
　　And help them with a lie or two additional,
I'm not to blame, as you well know — no more is
　　Any one else — they were become traditional;
Besides, their resurrection aids our glories
　　By contrast, which is what we just were wishing all:
And science profits by this resurrection —
Dead scandals form good subjects for dissection.

XXXII

Their friends had tried at reconciliation,
　　Then their relations, who made matters worse,
('Twere hard to tell upon a like occasion
　　To whom it may be best to have recourse —
I can't say much for friend or yet relation):
　　The lawyers did their utmost for divorce,
But scarce a fee was paid on either side
Before, unluckily, Don José died.

XXXIII

He died: and most unluckily, because,
    According to all hints I could collect
From counsel learned in those kinds of laws
    (Although their talk's obscure and circumspect),
His death contrived to spoil a charming cause;
    A thousand pities also with respect
To public feeling, which on this occasion
Was manifested in a great sensation.

XXXIV

But ah! he died; and buried with him lay
    The public feeling and the lawyers' fees:
His house was sold, his servants sent away,
    A Jew took one of his two mistresses,
A priest the other – at least so they say:
    I ask'd the doctors after his disease –
He died of the slow fever called the tertian,
And left his widow to her own aversion.

XXXV

Yet José was an honourable man,
　　That I must say, who knew him very well;
Therefore his frailties I'll no further scan,
　　Indeed there were not many more to tell:
And if his passions now and then outran
　　Discretion, and were not so peaceable
As Numa's (who was also named Pompilius),
He had been ill brought up, and was born bilious.

XXXVI

Whate'er might be his worthlessness or worth,
　　Poor fellow! he had many things to wound him,
Let's own – since it can do no good on earth –
　　It was a trying moment that which found him
Standing alone beside his desolate hearth,
　　Where all his household gods lay shiver'd round
　　　　him:
No choice was left his feelings or his pride,
Save death or Doctors' Commons – so he died.

XXXVII

Dying intestate, Juan was sole heir
   To a chancery suit, and messuages and lands,
Which, with a long minority and care,
   Promised to turn out well in proper hands:
Inez became sole guardian, which was fair,
   And answer'd but to nature's just demands;
An only son left with an only mother
Is brought up much more wisely than another.

XXXVIII

Sagest of women, even of widows, she
   Resolved that Juan should be quite a paragon,
And worthy of the noblest pedigree:
   (His sire was of Castile, his dam from Aragon).
Then for accomplishments of chivalry,
   In case our lord the king should go to war again,
He learn'd the arts of riding, fencing, gunnery,
And how to scale a fortress – or a nunnery.

XXXIX

But that which Donna Inez most desired,
    And saw into herself each day before all
The learned tutors whom for him she hired,
    Was, that his breeding should be strictly moral:
Much into all his studies she inquired,
    And so they were submitted first to her, all,
Arts, sciences, no branch was made a mystery
To Juan's eyes, excepting natural history.

XL

The languages, especially the dead,
    The sciences, and most of all the abstruse,
The arts, at least all such as could be said
    To be the most remote from common use,
In all these he was much and deeply read:
    But not a page of anything that's loose,
Or hints continuation of the species,
Was ever suffer'd, lest he should grow vicious.

XLI

His classic studies made a little puzzle,
  Because of filthy loves of gods and goddesses,
Who in the earlier ages raised a bustle,
  But never put on pantaloons or bodices;
His reverend tutors had at times a tussle,
  And for their Æneids, Iliads, and Odysseys,
Were forced to make an odd sort of apology,
For Donna Inez dreaded the Mythology.

XLII

Ovid's a rake, as half his verses show him,
  Anacreon's morals are a still worse sample,
Catullus scarcely has a decent poem,
  I don't think Sappho's Ode a good example,
Although Longinus tells us there is no hymn
  Where the sublime soars forth on wings more
    ample;
But Virgil's songs are pure, except that horrid one
Beginning with 'Formosum Pastor Corydon.'

XLIII

Lucretius' irreligion is too strong
    For early stomachs, to prove wholesome food;
I can't help thinking Juvenal was wrong,
    Although no doubt his real intent was good,
For speaking out so plainly in his song,
    So much indeed as to be downright rude;
And then what proper person can be partial
To all those nauseous epigrams of Martial?

XLIV

Juan was taught from out the best edition,
    Expurgated by learned men, who place,
Judiciously, from out the schoolboy's vision,
    The grosser parts; but, fearful to deface
Too much their modest bard by this omission,
    And pitying sore his mutilated case,
They only add them all in an appendix,
Which saves, in fact, the trouble of an index;

XLV

For there we have them all 'at one fell swoop,'
   Instead of being scatter'd through the pages;
They stand forth marshall'd in a handsome troop,
   To meet the ingenuous youth of future ages,
Till some less rigid editor shall stoop
   To call them back into their separate cages,
Instead of standing staring all together,
Like garden gods – and not so decent either.

XLVI

The Missal too (it was the family Missal)
   Was ornamented in a sort of way
Which ancient mass-books often are, and this all
   Kinds of grotesques illumined; and how they,
Who saw those figures on the margin kiss all,
   Could turn their optics to the text and pray,
Is more than I know – But Don Juan's mother
Kept this herself, and gave her son another.

XLVII

Sermons he read, and lectures he endured,
　　And homilies, and lives of all the saints;
To Jerome and to Chrysostom inured,
　　He did not take such studies for restraints;
But how faith is acquired, and then insured,
　　So well not one of the aforesaid paints
As Saint Augustine in his fine Confessions,
Which make the reader envy his transgressions.

XLVIII

This, too, was a seal'd book to little Juan —
　　I can't but say that his mamma was right,
If such an education was the true one.
　　She scarcely trusted him from out her sight;
Her maids were old, and if she took a new one,
　　You might be sure she was a perfect fright,
She did this during even her husband's life —
I recommend as much to every wife.

XLIX

Young Juan wax'd in godliness and grace;
   At six a charming child, and at eleven
With all the promise of as fine a face
   As e'er to man's maturer growth was given.
He studied steadily and grew apace,
   And seem'd, at least, in the right road to heaven,
For half his days were pass'd at church, the other
Between his tutors, confessor, and mother.

L

At six, I said, he was a charming child,
   At twelve he was a fine, but quiet boy;
Although in infancy a little wild,
   They tamed him down amongst them: to destroy
His natural spirit not in vain they toil'd,
   At least it seem'd so; and his mother's joy
Was to declare how sage, and still, and steady,
Her young philosopher was grown already.

LI

I had my doubts, perhaps I have them still,
    But what I say is neither here nor there:
I knew his father well, and have some skill
    In character – but it would not be fair
From sire to son to augur good or ill:
    He and his wife were an ill sorted pair –
But scandal's my aversion – I protest
Against all evil speaking, even in jest.

LII

For my part I say nothing – nothing – but
    This I will say – my reasons are my own –
That if I had an only son to put
    To school (as God be praised that I have none),
'Tis not with Donna Inez I would shut
    Him up to learn his catechism alone,
No – no – I'd send him out betimes to college,
For there it was I pick'd up my own knowledge.

LIII

For there one learns – 'tis not for me to boast,
    Though I acquired – but I pass over *that*,
As well as all the Greek I since have lost:
    I say that there's the place – but '*Verbum, sat,*'
I think I pick'd up too, as well as most,
    Knowledge of matters – but no matter *what* –
I never married – but, I think, I know
That sons should not be educated so.

LIV

Young Juan now was sixteen years of age,
    Tall, handsome, slender, but well knit: he seem'd
Active, though not so sprightly, as a page;
    And everybody but his mother deem'd
Him almost man; but she flew in a rage
    And bit her lips (for else she might have scream'd)
If any said so, for to be precocious
Was in her eyes a thing the most atrocious.

LV

Amongst her numerous acquaintance, all
    Selected for discretion and devotion,
There was the Donna Julia, whom to call
    Pretty were but to give a feeble notion
Of many charms in her as natural
    As sweetness to the flower, or salt to ocean,
Her zone to Venus, or his bow to Cupid
(But this last simile is trite and stupid).

LVI

The darkness of the Oriental eye
    Accorded with her Moorish origin;
(Her blood was not all Spanish, by the by;
    In Spain, you know, this is a sort of sin).
When proud Granada fell, and, forced to fly,
    Boabdil wept, of Donna Julia's kin
Some went to Africa, some stay'd in Spain,
Her great great grandmamma chose to remain.

LVII

She married (I forget the pedigree)
  With an Hidalgo, who transmitted down
His blood less noble than such blood should be;
  At such alliances his sires would frown,
In that point so precise in each degree
  That they bred *in and in*, as might be shown,
Marrying their cousins — nay, their aunts, and nieces,
Which always spoils the breed, if it increases.

LVIII

This heathenish cross restored the breed again,
  Ruin'd its blood, but much improved its flesh;
For from a root the ugliest in old Spain
  Sprung up a branch as beautiful as fresh;
The sons no more were short, the daughters plain:
  But there's a rumour which I fain would hush,
'Tis said that Donna Julia's grandmamma
Produced her Don more heirs at love than law.

LIX

However this might be, the race went on
    Improving still through every generation,
Until it centred in an only son,
    Who left an only daughter: my narration
May have suggested that this single one
    Could be but Julia (whom on this occasion
I shall have much to speak about), and she
Was married, charming, chaste, and twenty-three.

LX

Her eye (I'm very fond of handsome eyes)
    Was large and dark, suppressing half its fire
Until she spoke, then through its soft disguise
    Flash'd an expression more of pride than ire,
And love than either; and there would arise
    A something in them which was not desire,
But would have been, perhaps, but for the soul
Which struggled through and chasten'd down the
        whole.

LXI

Her glossy hair was cluster'd o'er a brow
    Bright with intelligence, and fair, and smooth;
Her eyebrow's shape was like the aërial bow,
    Her cheek all purple with the beam of youth,
Mounting, at times, to a transparent glow,
    As if her veins ran lightning; she, in sooth,
Possess'd an air and grace by no means common:
Her stature tall – I hate a dumpy woman.

LXII

Wedded she was some years, and to a man
    Of fifty, and such husbands are in plenty;
And yet, I think, instead of such a ONE
    'Twere better to have TWO of five-and-twenty,
Especially in countries near the sun:
    And now I think on't, 'mi vien in mente,'
Ladies even of the most uneasy virtue
Prefer a spouse whose age is short of thirty.

LXIII

'Tis a sad thing, I cannot choose but say,
    And all the fault of that indecent sun,
Who cannot leave alone our helpless clay,
    But will keep baking, broiling, burning on,
That howsoever people fast and pray,
    The flesh is frail, and so the soul undone:
What men call gallantry, and gods adultery,
Is much more common where the climate's sultry.

LXIV

Happy the nations of the moral North!
    Where all is virtue, and the winter season
Sends sin, without a rag on, shivering forth
    ('Twas snow that brought St. Anthony to reason);
Where juries cast up what a wife is worth,
    By laying whate'er sum, in mulct, they please on
The lover, who must pay a handsome price,
Because it is a marketable vice.

LXV

Alfonso was the name of Julia's lord,
  A man well looking for his years, and who
Was neither much beloved nor yet abhorr'd:
  They lived together as most people do,
Suffering each other's foibles by accord,
  And not exactly either *one* or *two*;
Yet he was jealous, though he did not show it,
For jealousy dislikes the world to know it.

LXVI

Julia was – yet I never could see why –
  With Donna Inez quite a favourite friend;
Between their tastes there was small sympathy,
  For not a line had Julia ever penn'd:
Some people whisper (but, no doubt, they lie,
  For malice still imputes some private end)
That Inez had, ere Don Alfonso's marriage,
Forgot with him her very prudent carriage;

LXVII

And that still keeping up the old connexion,
    Which time had lately render'd much more chaste,
She took his lady also in affection,
    And certainly this course was much the best:
She flatter'd Julia with her sage protection,
    And complimented Don Alfonso's taste;
And if she could not (who can?) silence scandal,
At least she left it a more slender handle.

LXVIII

I can't tell whether Julia saw the affair
    With other people's eyes, or if her own
Discoveries made, but none could be aware
    Of this, at least no symptom e'er was shown;
Perhaps she did not know, or did not care,
    Indifferent from the first, or callous grown:
I'm really puzzled what to think or say,
She kept her counsel in so close a way.

LXIX

Juan she saw, and, as a pretty child,
   Caress'd him often – such a thing might be
Quite innocently done, and harmless styled,
   When she had twenty years, and thirteen he;
But I am not so sure I should have smiled
   When he was sixteen, Julia twenty-three;
These few short years make wondrous alterations,
Particularly amongst sun-burnt nations.

LXX

Whate'er the cause might be, they had become
   Changed; for the dame grew distant, the youth shy,
Their looks cast down, their greetings almost dumb,
   And much embarrassment in either eye;
There surely will be little doubt with some
   That Donna Julia knew the reason why,
But as for Juan, he had no more notion
Than he who never saw the sea of ocean.

LXXI

Yet Julia's very coldness still was kind,
    And tremulously gentle her small hand
Withdrew itself from his, but left behind
    A little pressure, thrilling, and so bland
And slight, so very slight, that to the mind
    'Twas but a doubt; but ne'er magician's wand
Wrought change with all Armida's fairy art
Like what this light touch left on Juan's heart.

LXXII

And if she met him, though she smiled no more,
    She look'd a sadness sweeter than her smile,
As if her heart had deeper thoughts in store
    She must not own, but cherish'd more the while
For that compression in its burning core;
    Even innocence itself has many a wile,
And will not dare to trust itself with truth,
And love is taught hypocrisy from youth.

LXXIII

But passion most dissembles, yet betrays
    Even by its darkness; as the blackest sky
Foretells the heaviest tempest, it displays
    Its workings through the vainly guarded eye,
And in whatever aspect it arrays
    Itself, 'tis still the same hypocrisy:
Coldness or anger, even disdain or hate,
Are masks it often wears, and still too late.

LXXIV

Then there were sighs, the deeper for suppression,
    And stolen glances, sweeter for the theft,
And burning blushes, though for no transgression,
    Tremblings when met, and restlessness when left;
All these are little preludes to possession,
    Of which young passion cannot be bereft,
And merely tend to show how greatly love is
Embarrass'd at first starting with a novice.

LXXV

Poor Julia's heart was in an awkward state;
    She felt it going, and resolved to make
The noblest efforts for herself and mate,
    For honour's, pride's, religion's, virtue's sake.
Her resolutions were most truly great,
    And almost might have made a Tarquin quake:
She pray'd the Virgin Mary for her grace,
As being the best judge of a lady's case.

LXXVI

She vow'd she never would see Juan more,
    And next day paid a visit to his mother,
And look'd extremely at the opening door,
    Which, by the Virgin's grace, let in another;
Grateful she was, and yet a little sore –
    Again it opens, it can be no other,
'Tis surely Juan now – No! I'm afraid
That night the Virgin was no further pray'd.

LXXVII

She now determined that a virtuous woman
    Should rather face and overcome temptation,
That flight was base and dastardly, and no man
    Should ever give her heart the least sensation;
That is to say, a thought beyond the common
    Preference, that we must feel upon occasion,
For people who are pleasanter than others,
But then they only seem so many brothers.

LXXVIII

And even if by chance – and who can tell?
    The devil's so very sly – she should discover
That all within was not so very well,
    And, if still free, that such or such a lover
Might please perhaps, a virtuous wife can quell
    Such thoughts, and be the better when they're over;
And if the man should ask, 'tis but denial:
I recommend young ladies to make trial.

LXXIX

And then there are such things as love divine,
    Bright and immaculate, unmix'd and pure,
Such as the angels think so very fine,
    And matrons, who would be no less secure,
Platonic, perfect, 'just such love as mine':
    Thus Julia said – and thought so, to be sure;
And so I'd have her think, were I the man
On whom her reveries celestial ran.

LXXX

Such love is innocent, and may exist
    Between young persons without any danger:
A hand may first, and then a lip be kist;
    For my part, to such doings I'm a stranger,
But *hear* these freedoms form the utmost list
    Of all o'er which such love may be a ranger:
If people go beyond, 'tis quite a crime,
But not my fault – I tell them all in time.

LXXXI

Love, then, but love within its proper limits
    Was Julia's innocent determination
In young Don Juan's favour, and to him its
    Exertion might be useful on occasion;
And, lighted at too pure a shrine to dim its
    Ethereal lustre, with what sweet persuasion
He might be taught, by love and her together —
I really don't know what, nor Julia either.

LXXXII

Fraught with this fine intention, and well fenced
    In mail of proof — her purity of soul,
She, for the future of her strength convinced,
    And that her honour was a rock, or mole,
Exceeding sagely from that hour dispensed
    With any kind of troublesome control;
But whether Julia to the task was equal
Is that which must be mention'd in the sequel.

LXXXIII

Her plan she deem'd both innocent and feasible,
    And, surely, with a stripling of sixteen
Not scandal's fangs could fix on much that's seizable,
    Or if they did so, satisfied to mean
Nothing but what was good, her breast was peaceable:
    A quiet conscience makes one so serene!
Christians have burnt each other, quite persuaded
That all the Apostles would have done as they did.

LXXXIV

And if in the mean time her husband died,
    But Heaven forbid that such a thought should cross
Her brain, though in a dream! (and then she sigh'd)
    Never could she survive that common loss;
But just suppose that moment should betide,
    I only say suppose it – *inter nos.*
(This should be *entre nous*, for Julia thought
In French, but then the rhyme would go for nought.)

LXXXV

I only say, suppose this supposition:
  Juan being then grown up to man's estate
Would fully suit a widow of condition,
  Even seven years hence it would not be too late;
And in the interim (to pursue this vision)
  The mischief, after all, could not be great,
For he would learn the rudiments of love,
I mean the seraph way of those above.

LXXXVI

So much for Julia. Now we'll turn to Juan.
  Poor little fellow! he had no idea
Of his own case, and never hit the true one;
  In feelings quick as Ovid's Miss Medea,
He puzzled over what he found a new one,
  But not as yet imagined it could be a
Thing quite in course, and not at all alarming,
Which, with a little patience, might grow charming.

LXXXVII

Silent and pensive, idle, restless, slow,
  His home deserted for the lonely wood,
Tormented with a wound he could not know,
  His, like all deep grief, plunged in solitude:
I'm fond myself of solitude or so,
  But then, I beg it may be understood,
By solitude I mean a Sultan's, not
A hermit's, with a haram for a grot.

LXXXVIII

'Oh Love! in such a wilderness as this,
  Where transport and security entwine,
Here is the empire of thy perfect bliss,
  And here thou art a god indeed divine.'
The bard I quote from does not sing amiss,
  With the exception of the second line,
For that same twining 'transport and security'
Are twisted to a phrase of some obscurity.

LXXXIX

The poet meant, no doubt, and thus appeals
  To the good sense and senses of mankind,
The very thing which everybody feels,
  As all have found on trial, or may find,
That no one likes to be disturb'd at meals
  Or love. – I won't say more about 'entwined'
Or 'transport,' as we knew all that before,
But beg 'Security' will bolt the door.

XC

Young Juan wander'd by the glassy brooks,
  Thinking unutterable things; he threw
Himself at length within the leafy nooks
  Where the wild branch of the cork forest grew;
There poets find materials for their books,
  And every now and then we read them through,
So that their plan and prosody are eligible,
Unless, like Wordsworth, they prove unintelligible.

XCI

He, Juan (and not Wordsworth), so pursued
   His self-communion with his own high soul,
Until his mighty heart, in its great mood,
   Had mitigated part, though not the whole
Of its disease; he did the best he could
   With things not very subject to control,
And turn'd, without perceiving his condition,
Like Coleridge, into a metaphysician.

XCII

He thought about himself, and the whole earth,
   Of man the wonderful, and of the stars,
And how the deuce they ever could have birth;
   And then he thought of earthquakes, and of wars,
How many miles the moon might have in girth,
   Of air-balloons, and of the many bars
To perfect knowledge of the boundless skies; –
And then he thought of Donna Julia's eyes.

XCIII

In thoughts like these true wisdom may discern
    Longings sublime, and aspirations high,
Which some are born with, but the most part learn
    To plague themselves withal, they know not why:
'Twas strange that one so young should thus concern
    His brain about the action of the sky;
If *you* think 'twas philosophy that this did,
I can't help thinking puberty assisted.

XCIV

He pored upon the leaves, and on the flowers,
    And heard a voice in all the winds; and then
He thought of wood-nymphs and immortal bowers,
    And how the goddesses came down to men:
He miss'd the pathway, he forgot the hours,
    And when he look'd upon his watch again,
He found how much old Time had been a winner –
He also found that he had lost his dinner.

XCV

Sometimes he turn'd to gaze upon his book,
    Boscan, or Garcilasso; – by the wind
Even as the page is rustled while we look,
    So by the poesy of his own mind
Over the mystic leaf his soul was shook,
    As if 'twere one whereon magicians bind
Their spells, and give them to the passing gale
According to some good old woman's tale.

XCVI

Thus would he while his lonely hours away
    Dissatisfied, nor knowing what he wanted;
Nor glowing reverie, nor poet's lay,
    Could yield his spirit that for which it panted,
A bosom whereon he his head might lay,
    And hear the heart beat with the love it granted,
With—several other things, which I forget,
Or which, at least, I need not mention yet.

XCVII

Those lonely walks, and lengthening reveries,
  Could not escape the gentle Julia's eyes;
She saw that Juan was not at his ease;
  But that which chiefly may, and must surprise,
Is, that the Donna Inez did not tease
  Her only son with question or surmise;
Whether it was she did not see, or would not,
Or, like all very clever people, could not.

XCVIII

This may seem strange, but yet 'tis very common;
  For instance – gentlemen, whose ladies take
Leave to o'erstep the written rights of woman,
  And break the—Which commandment is't they
      break?
(I have forgot the number, and think no man
  Should rashly quote, for fear of a mistake.)
I say, when these same gentlemen are jealous,
They make some blunder, which their ladies tell us.

XCIX

A real husband always is suspicious,
    But still no less suspects in the wrong place,
Jealous of some one who had no such wishes,
    Or pandering blindly to his own disgrace,
By harbouring some dear friend extremely vicious;
    The last indeed's infallibly the case:
And when the spouse and friend are gone off wholly,
He wonders at their vice, and not his folly.

C

Thus parents also are at times short-sighted;
    Though watchful as the lynx, they ne'er discover,
The while the wicked world beholds delighted,
    Young Hopeful's mistress, or Miss Fanny's lover,
Till some confounded escapade has blighted
    The plan of twenty years, and all is over;
And then the mother cries, the father swears,
And wonders why the devil he got heirs.

CI

But Inez was so anxious, and so clear
  Of sight, that I must think, on this occasion,
She had some other motive much more near
  For leaving Juan to this new temptation,
But what that motive was, I shan't say here;
  Perhaps to finish Juan's education,
Perhaps to open Don Alfonso's eyes,
In case he thought his wife too great a prize.

CII

It was upon a day, a summer's day; —
  Summer's indeed a very dangerous season,
And so is spring about the end of May;
  The sun, no doubt, is the prevailing reason;
But whatso'er the cause is, one may say,
  And stand convicted of more truth than treason,
That there are months which nature grows more
      merry in, —
March has its hares, and May must have its heroine.

CIII

'Twas on a summer's day – the sixth of June: –
    I like to be particular in dates,
Not only of the age, and year, but moon;
    They are a sort of post-house, where the Fates
Change horses, making history change its tune,
    Then spur away o'er empires and o'er states,
Leaving at last not much besides chronology,
Excepting the post-obits of theology.

CIV

'Twas on the sixth of June, about the hour
    Of half-past six – perhaps still nearer seven –
When Julia sate within as pretty a bower
    As e'er held houri in that heathenish heaven
Described by Mahomet, and Anacreon Moore,
    To whom the lyre and laurels have been given,
With all the trophies of triumphant song –
He won them well, and may he wear them long!

CV

She sate, but not alone; I know not well
   How this same interview had taken place,
And even if I knew, I should not tell —
   People should hold their tongues in any case;
No matter how or why the thing befell,
   But there were she and Juan, face to face —
When two such faces are so, 'twould be wise,
But very difficult, to shut their eyes.

CVI

How beautiful she look'd! her conscious heart
   Glow'd in her cheek, and yet she felt no wrong,
Oh Love! how perfect is thy mystic art,
   Strengthening the weak, and trampling on the
      strong!
How self-deceitful is the sagest part
   Of mortals whom thy lure hath led along! —
The precipice she stood on was immense,
So was her creed in her own innocence.

CVII

She thought of her own strength, and Juan's youth,
    And of the folly of all prudish fears,
Victorious virtue, and domestic truth,
    And then of Don Alfonso's fifty years:
I wish these last had not occurr'd, in sooth,
    Because that number rarely much endears,
And through all climes, the snowy and the sunny,
Sounds ill in love, whate'er it may in money.

CVIII

When people say, 'I've told you *fifty* times,'
    They mean to scold, and very often do;
When poets say, 'I've written *fifty* rhymes,'
    They make you dread that they'll recite them too;
In gangs of *fifty*, thieves commit their crimes;
    At *fifty* love for love is rare, 'tis true,
But then, no doubt, it equally as true is,
A good deal may be bought for *fifty* Louis.

CIX

Julia had honour, virtue, truth, and love
    For Don Alfonso; and she inly swore,
By all the vows below to powers above,
    She never would disgrace the ring she wore,
Nor leave a wish which wisdom might reprove;
    And while she ponder'd this, besides much more,
One hand on Juan's carelessly was thrown,
Quite by mistake – she thought it was her own;

CX

Unconsciously she lean'd upon the other,
    Which play'd within the tangles of her hair;
And to contend with thoughts she could not smother
    She seem'd, by the distraction of her air.
'Twas surely very wrong in Juan's mother
    To leave together this imprudent pair,
She who for many years had watch'd her son so –
I'm very certain *mine* would not have done so.

CXI

The hand which still held Juan's, by degrees
    Gently, but palpably confirm'd its grasp,
As if it said, 'Detain me, if you please';
    Yet there's no doubt she only meant to clasp
His fingers with a pure Platonic squeeze;
    She would have shrunk as from a toad, or asp,
Had she imagined such a thing could rouse
A feeling dangerous to a prudent spouse.

CXII

I cannot know what Juan thought of this,
    But what he did, is much what you would do;
His young lip thank'd it with a grateful kiss,
    And then, abash'd at its own joy, withdrew
In deep despair, lest he had done amiss, –
    Love is so very timid when 'tis new:
She blush'd, and frown'd not, but she strove to speak,
And held her tongue, her voice was grown so weak.

CXIII

The sun set, and up rose the yellow moon:
    The devil's in the moon for mischief; they
Who call'd her CHASTE, methinks, began too soon
    Their nomenclature; there is not a day,
The longest, not the twenty-first of June,
    Sees half the business in a wicked way,
On which three single hours of moonshine smile –
And then she looks so modest all the while.

CXIV

There is a dangerous silence in that hour,
    A stillness, which leaves room for the full soul
To open all itself, without the power
    Of calling wholly back its self-control;
The silver light which, hallowing tree and tower,
    Sheds beauty and deep softness o'er the whole,
Breathes also to the heart, and o'er it throws
A loving languor, which is not repose.

CXV

And Julia sate with Juan, half embraced
    And half retiring from the glowing arm,
Which trembled like the bosom where 'twas placed;
    Yet still she must have thought there was no harm,
Or else 'twere easy to withdraw her waist;
    But then the situation had its charm,
And then——God knows what next – I can't go on;
I'm almost sorry that I e'er begun.

CXVI

Oh Plato! Plato! you have paved the way,
    With your confounded fantasies, to more
Immoral conduct by the fancied sway
    Your system feigns o'er the controlless core
Of human hearts, than all the long array
    Of poets and romancers: – You're a bore,
A charlatan, a coxcomb – and have been,
At best, no better than a go-between.

CXVII

And Julia's voice was lost, except in sighs,
    Until too late for useful conversation;
The tears were gushing from her gentle eyes,
    I wish, indeed, they had not had occasion;
But who, alas! can love, and then be wise?
    Not that remorse did not oppose temptation;
A little still she strove, and much repented,
And whispering 'I will ne'er consent' – consented.

CXVIII

'Tis said that Xerxes offer'd a reward
    To those who could invent him a new pleasure.
Methinks the requisition's rather hard,
    And must have cost his majesty a treasure:
For my part, I'm a moderate-minded bard,
    Fond of a little love (which I call leisure);
I care not for new pleasures, as the old
Are quite enough for me, so they but hold.

CXIX

Oh Pleasure! you're indeed a pleasant thing,
    Although one must be damn'd for you, no doubt:
I make a resolution every spring
    Of reformation, ere the year run out,
But somehow, this my vestal vow takes wing,
    Yet still, I trust, it may be kept throughout:
I'm very sorry, very much ashamed,
And mean, next winter, to be quite reclaim'd.

CXX

Here my chaste Muse a liberty must take –
    Start not! still chaster reader – she'll be nice hence-
Forward, and there is no great cause to quake;
    This liberty is a poetic licence,
Which some irregularity may make
    In the design, and as I have a high sense
Of Aristotle and the Rules, 'tis fit
To beg his pardon when I err a bit.

CXXI

This licence is to hope the reader will
    Suppose from June the sixth (the fatal day
Without whose epoch my poetic skill
    For want of facts would all be thrown away),
But keeping Julia and Don Juan still
    In sight, that several months have pass'd; we'll say
'Twas in November, but I'm not so sure
About the day – the era's more obscure.

CXXII

We'll talk of that anon. – 'Tis sweet to hear
    At midnight on the blue and moonlit deep
The song and oar of Adria's gondolier,
    By distance mellow'd, o'er the waters sweep;
'Tis sweet to see the evening star appear;
    'Tis sweet to listen as the night-winds creep
From leaf to leaf; 'tis sweet to view on high
The rainbow, based on ocean, span the sky.

CXXIII

'Tis sweet to hear the watch-dog's honest bark
  Bay deep-mouth'd welcome as we draw near home;
'Tis sweet to know there is an eye will mark
  Our coming, and look brighter when we come;
'Tis sweet to be awaken'd by the lark,
  Or lull'd by falling waters; sweet the hum
Of bees, the voice of girls, the song of birds,
The lisp of children, and their earliest words.

CXXIV

Sweet is the vintage, when the showering grapes
  In Bacchanal profusion reel to earth,
Purple and gushing; sweet are our escapes
  From civic revelry to rural mirth;
Sweet to the miser are his glittering heaps,
  Sweet to the father is his first-born's birth,
Sweet is revenge – especially to women,
Pillage to soldiers, prize-money to seamen.

CXXV

Sweet is a legacy, and passing sweet
  The unexpected death of some old lady
Or gentleman of seventy years complete,
  Who've made 'us youth' wait too – too long already
For an estate, or cash, or country seat,
  Still breaking, but with stamina so steady
That all the Israelites are fit to mob its
Next owner for their double-damn'd post-obits.

CXXVI

'Tis sweet to win, no matter how, one's laurels,
  By blood or ink; 'tis sweet to put an end
To strife; 'tis sometimes sweet to have our quarrels,
  Particularly with a tiresome friend:
Sweet is old wine in bottles, ale in barrels;
  Dear is the helpless creature we defend
Against the world; and dear the schoolboy spot
We ne'er forget, though there we are forgot.

CXXVII

But sweeter still than this, than these, than all,
   Is first and passionate love — it stands alone,
Like Adam's recollection of his fall;
   The tree of knowledge has been pluck'd — all's
     known —
And life yields nothing further to recall
   Worthy of this ambrosial sin, so shown,
No doubt in fable, as the unforgiven
Fire which Prometheus filch'd for us from heaven.

CXXVIII

Man's a strange animal, and makes strange use
   Of his own nature, and the various arts,
And likes particularly to produce
   Some new experiment to show his parts;
This is the age of oddities let loose,
   Where different talents find their different marts;
You'd best begin with truth, and when you've lost your
Labour, there's a sure market for imposture.

192

CXXIX

What opposite discoveries we have seen!
  (Signs of true genius, and of empty pockets.)
One makes new noses, one a guillotine,
    One breaks your bones, one sets them in their
      sockets;
But vaccination certainly has been
  A kind antithesis to Congreve's rockets,
With which the Doctor paid off an old pox,
By borrowing a new one from an ox.

CXXX

Bread has been made (indifferent) from potatoes;
  And galvanism has set some corpses grinning,
But has not answer'd like the apparatus
  Of the Humane Society's beginning,
By which men are unsuffocated gratis:
  What wondrous new machines have late been
    spinning!
I said the small pox has gone out of late;
Perhaps it may be follow'd by the great.

CXXXI

'Tis said the great came from America;
    Perhaps it may set out on its return, –
The population there so spreads, they say
    'Tis grown high time to thin it in its turn,
With war, or plague, or famine, any way,
    So that civilisation they may learn;
And which in ravage the more loathsome evil is –
Their real lues, or our pseudo-syphilis?

CXXXII

This is the patent age of new inventions
    For killing bodies, and for saving souls,
All propagated with the best intentions;
    Sir Humphry Davy's lantern, by which coals
Are safely mined for in the mode he mentions,
    Tombuctoo travels, voyages to the Poles,
Are ways to benefit mankind, as true,
Perhaps, as shooting them at Waterloo.

CXXXIII

Man's a phenomenon, one knows not what,
    And wonderful beyond all wondrous measure;
'Tis pity though, in this sublime world, that
    Pleasure's a sin, and sometimes sin's a pleasure;
Few mortals know what end they woud be at,
    But whether glory, power, or love, or treasure,
The path is through perplexing ways, and when
The goal is gain'd, we die, you know – and then—

CXXXIV

What then? – I do not know, no more do you –
    And so good night. – Return we to our story:
'Twas in November, when fine days are few,
    And the far mountains wax a little hoary,
And clap a white cape on their mantles blue;
    And the sea dashes round the promontory,
And the loud breaker boils against the rock,
And sober suns must set at five o'clock.

CXXXV

'Twas, as the watchmen say, a cloudy night;
   No moon, no stars, the wind was low or loud
By gusts, and many a sparkling hearth was bright
   With the piled wood, round which the family crowd;
There's something cheerful in that sort of light,
   Even as a summer sky's without a cloud:
I'm fond of fire, and crickets, and all that,
A lobster salad, and champagne, and chat.

CXXXVI

'Twas midnight – Donna Julia was in bed,
   Sleeping, most probably, – when at her door
Arose a clatter might awake the dead,
   If they had never been awoke before,
And that they have been so we all have read,
   And are to be so, at the least, once more; –
The door was fasten'd, but with voice and fist
First knocks were heard, then 'Madam – Madam – hist!

CXXXVII

'For God's sake, Madam – Madam – here's my master,
    With more than half the city at his back –
Was ever heard of such a curst disaster!
    'Tis not my fault – I kept good watch – Alack!
Do pray undo the bolt a little faster –
    They're on the stair just now, and in a crack
Will all be here; perhaps he yet may fly –
Surely the window's not so *very* high!'

CXXXVIII

By this time Don Alfonso was arrived,
    With torches, friends, and servants in great number;
The major part of them had long been wived,
    And therefore paused not to disturb the slumber
Of any wicked woman, who contrived
    By stealth her husband's temples to encumber:
Examples of this kind are so contagious,
Were *one* not punish'd, *all* would be outrageous.

CXXXIX

I can't tell how, or why, or what suspicion
    Could enter into Don Alfonso's head;
But for a cavalier of his condition
    It surely was exceedingly ill-bred,
Without a word of previous admonition,
    To hold a levee round his lady's bed,
And summon lackeys, arm'd with fire and sword,
To prove himself the thing he most abhorr'd.

CXL

Poor Donna Julia! starting as from sleep
    (Mind – that I do not say – she had not slept),
Began at once to scream, and yawn, and weep;
    Her maid, Antonia, who was an adept,
Contrived to fling the bed-clothes in a heap,
    As if she had just now from out them crept:
I can't tell why she should take all this trouble
To prove her mistress had been sleeping double.

CXLI

But Julia mistress, and Antonia maid,
   Appear'd like two poor harmless women, who
Of goblins, but still more of men afraid,
   Had thought one man might be deterr'd by two,
And therefore side by side were gently laid,
   Until the hours of absence should run through,
And truant husband should return, and say,
'My dear, I was the first who came away.'

CXLII

Now Julia found at length a voice, and cried,
   'In heaven's name, Don Alfonso, what d'ye mean?
Has madness seized you? would that I had died
   Ere such a monster's victim I had been!
What may this midnight violence betide,
   A sudden fit of drunkenness or spleen?
Dare you suspect me, whom the thought would kill?
Search, then, the room!' – Alfonso said, 'I will.'

CXLIII

He search'd, *they* search'd, and rummaged everywhere,
  Closet and clothes-press, chest and window-seat,
And found much linen, lace, and several pair
  Of stockings, slippers, brushes, combs, complete,
With other articles of ladies fair,
  To keep them beautiful, or leave them neat:
Arras they prick'd and curtains with their swords,
And wounded several shutters, and some boards.

CXLIV

Under the bed they search'd, and there they found —
  No matter what — it was not that they sought;
They open'd windows, gazing if the ground
  Had signs or footmarks, but the earth said nought;
And then they stared each other's faces round:
  'Tis odd, not one of all these seekers thought,
And seems to me almost a sort of blunder,
Of looking *in* the bed as well as under.

CXLV

During this inquisition Julia's tongue
    Was not asleep – 'Yes, search and search,' she cried,
'Insult on insult heap, and wrong on wrong!
    It was for this that I became a bride!
For this in silence I have suffer'd long
    A husband like Alfonso at my side;
But now I'll bear no more, nor here remain,
If there be law or lawyers in all Spain.

CXLVI

'Yes, Don Alfonso! husband now no more,
    If ever you indeed deserved the name,
Is't worthy of your years? – you have threescore –
    Fifty, or sixty, it is all the same –
Is't wise or fitting, causeless to explore
    For facts against a virtuous woman's fame?
Ungrateful, perjured, barbarous Don Alfonso,
How dare you think your lady would go on so?

CXLVII

'Is it for this I have disdain'd to hold
      The common privileges of my sex?
That I have chosen a confessor so old
      And deaf, that any other it would vex,
And never once he has had cause to scold,
      But found my very innocence perplex
So much, he always doubted I was married —
How sorry you will be when I've miscarried!

CXLVIII

'Was it for this that no Cortejo e'er
      I yet have chosen from out the youth of Seville?
Is it for this I scarce went anywhere,
      Except to bull-fights, mass, play, rout, and revel?
Is it for this, whate'er my suitors were,
      I favour'd none — nay, was almost uncivil?
Is it for this that General Count O'Reilly,
Who took Algiers, declares I used him vilely?

CXLIX

'Did not the Italian Musico Cazzani
    Sing at my heart six months at least in vain?
Did not his countryman, Count Corniani,
    Call me the only virtuous wife in Spain?
Were there not also Russians, English, many?
    The Count Strongstroganoff I put in pain,
And Lord Mount Coffeehouse, the Irish peer,
Who kill'd himself for love (with wine) last year.

CL

'Have I not had two bishops at my feet?
    The Duke of Ichar, and Don Fernan Nunez?
And is it thus a faithful wife you treat?
    I wonder in what quarter now the moon is:
I praise your vast forbearance not to beat
    Me also, since the time so opportune is –
Oh, valiant man! with sword drawn and cock'd trigger,
Now, tell me, don't you cut a pretty figure?

CLI

'Was it for this you took your sudden journey,
　　Under pretence of business indispensable,
With that sublime of rascals your attorney,
　　Whom I see standing there, and looking sensible
Of having play'd the fool? though both I spurn, he
　　Deserves the worst, his conduct's less defensible,
Because, no doubt, 'twas for his dirty fee,
And not from any love to you nor me.

CLII

'If he comes here to take a deposition,
　　By all means let the gentleman proceed;
You've made the apartment in a fit condition: –
　　There's pen and ink for you, sir, when you need –
Let everything be noted with precision,
　　I would not you for nothing should be fee'd –
But as my maid's undrest, pray turn your spies out.'
'Oh!' sobb'd Antonia, 'I could tear their eyes out.'

CLIII

'There is the closet, there the toilet, there
  The antechamber – search them under, over;
There is the sofa, there the great armchair,
  The chimney – which would really hold a lover.
I wish to sleep, and beg you will take care
  And make no further noise, till you discover
The secret cavern of this lurking treasure –
And when 'tis found, let me, too, have that pleasure.

CLIV

'And now, Hidalgo! now that you have thrown
  Doubt upon me, confusion over all,
Pray have the courtesy to make it known
  Who is the man you search for? how d'ye call
Him? what's his lineage? let him but be shown –
  I hope he's young and handsome – is he tall?
Tell me – and be assured, that since you stain
Mine honour thus, it shall not be in vain.

CLV

'At least, perhaps, he has not sixty years,
    At that age he would be too old for slaughter,
Or for so young a husband's jealous fears –
    (Antonia! let me have a glass of water.)
I am ashamed of having shed these tears,
    ·They are unworthy of my father's daughter;
My mother dream'd not in my natal hour,
That I should fall into a monster's power.

CLVI

'Perhaps 'tis of Antonia you are jealous,
    You saw that she was sleeping by my side,
When you broke in upon us with your fellows;
    Look where you please – we've nothing, sir, to hide;
Only another time, I trust, you'll tell us,
    Or for the sake of decency abide
A moment at the door, that we may be
Drest to receive so much good company.

CLVII

'And now, sir, I have done, and say no more;
    The little I have said may serve to show
The guileless heart in silence may grieve o'er
    The wrongs to whose exposure it is slow: –
I leave you to your conscience as before,
    'Twill one day ask you, *why* you used me so?
God grant you feel not then the bitterest grief!
Antonia! where's my pocket-handkerchief?'

CLVIII

She ceased, and turn'd upon her pillow; pale
    She lay, her dark eyes flashing through their tears,
Like skies that rain and lighten; as a veil,
    Waved and o'ershading her wan cheek, appears
Her streaming hair; the black curls strive, but fail,
    To hide the glossy shoulder, which uprears
Its snow through all; – her soft lips lie apart,
And louder than her breathing beats her heart.

CLIX

The Senhor Don Alfonso stood confused;
    Antonia bustled round the ransack'd room,
And, turning up her nose, with looks abused
    Her master, and his myrmidons, of whom
Not one, except the attorney, was amused;
    He, like Achates, faithful to the tomb,
So there were quarrels, cared not for the cause,
Knowing they must be settled by the laws.

CLX

With prying snub-nose, and small eyes, he stood,
    Following Antonia's motions here and there,
With much suspicion in his attitude;
    For reputations he had little care;
So that a suit or action were made good,
    Small pity had he for the young and fair,
And ne'er believed in negatives, till these
Were proved by competent false witnesses.

CLXI

But Don Alfonso stood with downcast looks,
    And, truth to say, he made a foolish figure;
When, after searching in five hundred nooks,
    And treating a young wife with so much rigour,
He gain'd no point, except some self-rebukes,
    Added to those his lady with such vigour
Had pour'd upon him for the last half hour,
Quick, thick, and heavy – as a thunder-shower.

CLXII

At first he tried to hammer an excuse,
    To which the sole reply were tears and sobs,
And indications of hysterics, whose
    Prologue is always certain throes, and throbs,
Gasps, and whatever else the owners choose:
    Alfonso saw his wife, and thought of Job's;
He saw too, in perspective, her relations,
And then he tried to muster all his patience.

CLXIII

He stood in act to speak, or rather stammer,
　　But sage Antonia cut him short before
The anvil of his speech received the hammer,
　　With 'Pray, sir, leave the room, and say no more,
Or madam dies.' – Alfonso mutter'd, 'D – n her,'
　　But nothing else, the time of words was o'er;
He cast a rueful look or two, and did,
He knew not wherefore, that which he was bid.

CLXIV

With him retired his *'posse comitatus,'*
　　The attorney last, who linger'd near the door
Reluctantly, still tarrying there as late as
　　Antonia let him – not a little sore
At this most strange and unexplain'd *'hiatus'*
　　In Don Alfonso's facts, which just now wore
An awkward look; as he revolved the case,
The door was fasten'd in his legal face.

CLXV

No sooner was it bolted, than – O shame!
  Oh sin! Oh sorrow! and Oh womankind!
How can you do such things and keep your fame,
  Unless this world, and t'other too, be blind?
Nothing so dear as an unfilch'd good name!
  But to proceed – for there is more behind:
With much heartfelt reluctance be it said,
Young Juan slipp'd, half-smother'd, from the bed.

CLXVI

He had been hid – I don't pretend to say
  How, nor can I indeed describe the where –
Young, slender, and pack'd easily, he lay,
  No doubt, in little compass, round or square;
But pity him I neither must nor may
  His suffocation by that pretty pair;
'Twere better, sure, to die so, than be shut
With maudlin Clarence in his Malmsey butt.

CLXVII

And, secondly, I pity not, because
　　He had no business to commit a sin,
Forbid by heavenly, fined by human laws;
　　At least 'twas rather early to begin;
But at sixteen the conscience rarely gnaws
　　So much as when we call our old debts in
At sixty years, and draw the accompts of evil,
And find a deuced balance with the devil.

CLXVIII

Of his position I can give no notion;
　　'Tis written in the Hebrew Chronicle,
How the physicians, leaving pill and potion,
　　Prescribed, by way of blister, a young belle,
When old King David's blood grew dull in motion,
　　And that the medicine answer'd very well;
Perhaps 'twas in a different way applied,
For David lived, but Juan nearly died.

CLXIX

What's to be done? Alfonso will be back
    The moment he has sent his fools away.
Antonia's skill was put upon the rack,
    But no device could be brought into play –
And how to parry the renew'd attack?
    Besides, it wanted but few hours of day:
Antonia puzzled; Julia did not speak,
But press'd her bloodless lip to Juan's cheek.

CLXX

He turn'd his lip to hers, and with his hand
    Call'd back the tangles of her wandering hair;
Even then their love they could not all command,
    And half forgot their danger and despair:
Antonia's patience now was at a stand –
    'Come, come, 'tis no time now for fooling there,'
She whisper'd, in great wrath – 'I must deposit
This pretty gentleman within the closet:

CLXXI

'Pray, keep your nonsense for some luckier night –
  Who can have put my master in this mood?
What will become on't – I'm in such a fright,
  The devil's in the urchin, and no good –
Is this a time for giggling? this a plight?
  Why, don't you know that it may end in blood?
You'll lose your life, and I shall lose my place,
My mistress all, for that half-girlish face.

CLXXII

'Had it but been for a stout cavalier
  Of twenty-five or thirty – (come, make haste)
But for a child, what piece of work is here!
  I really, madam, wonder at your taste –
(Come, sir, get in) – my master must be near:
  There, for the present, at the least, he's fast,
And if we can but till the morning keep
Our counsel – (Juan, mind, you must not sleep).'

CLXXIII

Now, Don Alfonso entering, but alone,
   Closed the oration of the trusty maid:
She loiter'd, and he told her to be gone,
   An order somewhat sullenly obey'd;
However, present remedy was none,
   And no great good seem'd answer'd if she staid;
Regarding both with slow and sidelong view,
She snuff'd the candle, curtsied, and withdrew.

CLXXIV

Alfonso paused a minute — then begun
   Some strange excuses for his late proceeding:
He would not justify what he had done,
   To say the best, it was extreme ill-breeding;
But there were ample reasons for it, none
   Of which he specified in this his pleading:
His speech was a fine sample, on the whole,
Of rhetoric, which the learn'd call *'rigmarole.'*

CLXXV

Julia said nought; though all the while there rose
    A ready answer, which at once enables
A matron, who her husband's foible knows,
    By a few timely words to turn the tables,
Which, if it does not silence, still must pose, –
    Even if it should comprise a pack of fables;
'Tis to retort with firmness, and when he
Suspects with *one*, do you reproach with *three*.

CLXXVI

Julia, in fact, had tolerable grounds, –
    Alfonso's loves with Inez were well known;
But whether 'twas that one's own guilt confounds –
    But that can't be, as has been often shown,
A lady with apologies abounds; –
    It might be that her silence sprang alone
From delicacy to Don Juan's ear,
To whom she knew his mother's fame was dear.

CLXXVII

There might be one more motive, which makes two,
　　Alfonso ne'er to Juan had alluded, –
Mentioned his jealousy, but never who
　　Had been the happy lover, he concluded,
Conceal'd amongst his premises; 'tis true,
　　His mind the more o'er this its mystery brooded
To speak of Inez now were, one may say,
Like throwing Juan in Alfonso's way.

CLXXVIII

A hint, in tender cases, is enough;
　　Silence is best: besides there is a *tact* –
(That modern phrase appears to me sad stuff,
　　But it will serve to keep my verse compact) –
Which keeps, when push'd by questions rather rough,
　　A lady always distant from the fact:
The charming creatures lie with such a grace,
There's nothing so becoming to the face.

CLXXIX

They blush, and we believe them, at least I
  Have always done so; 'tis of no great use,
In any case, attempting a reply,
  For then their eloquence grows quite profuse;
And when at length they're out of breath, they sigh,
  And cast their languid eyes down, and let loose
A tear or two, and then we make it up;
And then – and then – and then – sit down and sup.

CLXXX

Alfonso closed his speech, and begg'd her pardon,
  Which Julia half withheld, and then half granted,
And laid conditions, he thought very hard, on,
  Denying several little things he wanted:
He stood like Adam lingering near his garden,
  With useless penitence perplex'd and haunted,
Beseeching she no further would refuse,
When, lo! he stumbled o'er a pair of shoes.

CLXXXI

A pair of shoes! – what then? not much, if they
    Are such as fit with ladies' feet, but these
(No one can tell how much I grieve to say)
    Were masculine; to see them, and to seize,
Was but a moment's act. – Ah! well-a-day!
    My teeth begin to chatter, my veins freeze –
Alfonso first examined well their fashion,
And then flew out into another passion.

CLXXXII

He left the room for his relinquish'd sword,
    And Julia instant to the closet flew.
'Fly, Juan, fly! for heaven's sake – not a word –
    The door is open – you may yet slip through
The passage you so often have explored –
    Here is the garden-key – Fly – fly – Adieu!
Haste – haste! I hear Alfonso's hurrying feet –
Day has not broke – there's no one in the street.'

CLXXXIII

None can say that this was not good advice,
    The only mischief was, it came too late;
Of all experience 'tis the usual price,
    A sort of income-tax laid on by fate:
Juan had reach'd the room-door in a trice,
    And might have done so by the garden-gate,
But met Alfonso in his dressing-gown,
Who threaten'd death – so Juan knock'd him down.

CLXXXIV

Dire was the scuffle, and out went the light;
    Antonia cried out 'Rape!' and Julia 'Fire!'
But not a servant stirr'd to aid the fight.
    Alfonso, pommell'd to his heart's desire,
Swore lustily he'd be revenged this night;
    And Juan, too, blasphemed an octave higher;
His blood was up: though young, he was a Tartar,
And not at all disposed to prove a martyr.

CLXXXV

Alfonso's sword had dropp'd ere he could draw it,
    And they continued battling hand to hand,
For Juan very luckily ne'er saw it;
    His temper not being under great command,
If at that moment he had chanced to claw it,
    Alfonso's days had not been in the land
Much longer. – Think of husbands', lovers' lives!
And how ye may be doubly widows – wives!

CLXXXVI

Alfonso grappled to detain the foe,
    And Juan throttled him to get away,
And blood ('twas from the nose) began to flow;
    At last, as they more faintly wrestling lay,
Juan contrived to give an awkward blow,
    And then his only garment quite gave way;
He fled, like Joseph, leaving it; but there,
I doubt, all likeness ends between the pair.

CLXXXVII

Lights came at length, and men, and maids, who found
    An awkward spectacle their eyes before;
Antonia in hysterics, Julia swoon'd,
    Alfonso leaning, breathless, by the door;
Some half-torn drapery scatter'd on the ground,
    Some blood, and several footsteps, but no more:
Juan the gate gain'd, turn'd the key about,
And liking not the inside, lock'd the out.

CLXXXVIII

Here ends this canto. – Need I sing, or say,
    How Juan, naked, favour'd by the night,
Who favours what she should not, found his way,
    And reach'd his home in an unseemly plight?
The pleasant scandal which arose next day,
    The nine days' wonder which was brought to light,
And how Alfonso sued for a divorce,
Were in the English newspapers, of course.

CLXXXIX

If you would like to see the whole proceedings,
    The depositions and the cause at full,
The names of all the witnesses, the pleadings
    Of counsel to nonsuit, or to annul,
There's more than one edition, and the readings
    Are various, but they none of them are dull;
The best is that in short-hand ta'en by Gurney,
Who to Madrid on purpose made a journey.

CXC

But Donna Inez, to divert the train
    Of one of the most circulating scandals
That had for centuries been known in Spain,
    At least since the retirement of the Vandals,
First vow'd (and never had she vow'd in vain)
    To Virgin Mary several pounds of candles;
And then, by the advice of some old ladies,
She sent her son to be shipp'd off from Cadiz.

CXCI

She had resolved that he should travel through
    All European climes, by land or sea,
To mend his former morals, and get new,
    Especially in France and Italy
(At least this is the thing most people do).
    Julia was sent into a convent: she
Grieved, but perhaps, her feelings may be better
Shown in the following copy of her Letter: —

CXCII

'They tell me 'tis decided; you depart:
    'Tis wise — 'tis well, but not the less a pain;
I have no further claim on your young heart,
    Mine is the victim, and would be again:
To love too much has been the only art
    I used; — I write in haste, and if a stain
Be on this sheet, 'tis not what it appears;
My eyeballs burn and throb, but have no tears.

CXCIII

'I loved, I love you, for this love have lost
　　State, station, heaven, mankind's, my own esteem,
And yet cannot regret what it hath cost,
　　So dear is still the memory of that dream;
Yet, if I name my guilt, 'tis not to boast,
　　None can deem harshlier of me than I deem:
I trace this scrawl because I cannot rest –
I've nothing to reproach or to request.

CXCIV

'Man's love is of man's life a thing apart,
　　'Tis woman's whole existence; man may range
The court, camp, church, the vessel, and the mart;
　　Sword, gown, gain, glory, offer in exchange
Pride, fame, ambition, to fill up his heart,
　　And few there are whom these cannot estrange;
Men have all these resources, we but one,
To love again, and be again undone.

CXCV

'You will proceed in pleasure, and in pride,
    Beloved and loving many; all is o'er
For me on earth, except some years to hide
    My shame and sorrow deep in my heart's core:
These I could bear, but cannot cast aside
    The passion which still rages as before, –
And so farewell – forgive me, love me – No,
That word is idle now – but let it go.

CXCVI

'My breast has been all weakness, is so yet;
    But still I think I can collect my mind;
My blood still rushes where my spirit's set,
    As roll the waves before the settled wind;
My heart is feminine, nor can forget –
    To all, except one image, madly blind;
So shakes the needle, and so stands the pole,
As vibrates my fond heart to my fix'd soul.

CXCVII

'I have no more to say, but linger still,
   And dare not set my seal upon this sheet,
And yet I may as well the task fulfil.
   My misery can scarce be more complete:
I had not lived till now, could sorrow kill;
   Death shuns the wretch who fain the blow would
      meet,
And I must even survive this last adieu,
And bear with life to love and pray for you!'

CXCVIII

This note was written upon gilt-edged paper
   With a neat little crow-quill, slight and new;
Her small white hand could hardly reach the taper,
   It trembled as magnetic needles do,
And yet she did not let one tear escape her;
   The seal a sun-flower; *'Elle vous suit partout,'*
The motto, cut upon a white cornelian;
The wax was superfine, its hue vermilion.

CXCIX

This was Don Juan's earliest scrape; but whether
    I shall proceed with his adventures is
Dependent on the public altogether;
    We'll see, however, what they say to this,
Their favour in an author's cap's a feather,
    And no great mischief's done by their caprice;
And if their approbation we experience,
Perhaps they'll have some more about a year hence.

CC

My poem's epic, and is meant to be
    Divided in twelve books; each book containing,
With love, and war, a heavy gale at sea,
    A list of ships, and captains, and kings reigning,
New characters; the episodes are three:
    A panoramic view of hell's in training,
After the style of Virgil and of Homer,
So that my name of Epic's no misnomer.

CCI

All these things will be specified in time,
    With strict regard to Aristotle's rules,
The *Vade Mecum* of the true sublime,
    Which makes so many poets, and some fools:
Prose poets like blank-verse, I'm fond of rhyme,
    Good workmen never quarrel with their tools;
I've got new mythological machinery,
And very handsome supernatural scenery.

CCII

There's only one slight difference between
    Me and my epic brethren gone before,
And here the advantage is my own, I ween
    (Not that I have not several merits more,
But this will more peculiarly be seen);
    They so embellish, that 'tis quite a bore
Their labyrinth of fables to thread through,
Whereas this story's actually true.

CCIII

If any person doubt it, I appeal
    To history, tradition, and to facts,
To newspapers, whose truth all know and feel,
    To plays in five, and operas in three acts;
All these confirm my statement a good deal,
    But that which more completely faith extracts
Is, that myself, and several now in Seville,
Saw Juan's last elopement with the devil.

CCIV

If ever I should condescend to prose,
    I'll write poetical commandments, which
Shall supersede beyond all doubt all those
    That went before; in these I shall enrich
My text with many things that no one knows,
    And carry precept to the highest pitch:
I'll call the work 'Longinus o'er a Bottle,
Or, Every Poet his *own* Aristotle.'

CCV

Thou shalt believe in Milton, Dryden, Pope;
    Thou shalt not set up Wordsworth, Coleridge,
        Southey;
Because the first is crazed beyond all hope,
    The second drunk, the third so quaint and mouthy:
With Crabbe it may be difficult to cope,
    And Campbell's Hippocrene is somewhat drouthy:
Thou shalt not steal from Samuel Rogers, nor
Commit – flirtation with the muse of Moore.

CCVI

Thou shalt not covet Mr. Sotheby's Muse,
    His Pegasus, nor anything that's his;
Thou shalt not bear false witness like 'the Blues' –
    (There's *one*, at least, is very fond of this);
Thou shalt not write, in short, but what I choose;
    This is true criticism, and you may kiss –
Exactly as you please, or not, – the rod;
But if you don't, I'll lay it on, by G –d!

CCVII

If any person should presume to assert
    This story is not moral, first, I pray,
That they will not cry out before they're hurt,
    Then that they'll read it o'er again, and say
(But, doubtless, nobody will be so pert),
    That this is not a moral tale, though gay;
Besides, in Canto Twelfth, I mean to show
The very place where wicked people go.

CCVIII

If, after all, there should be some so blind
    To their own good this warning to despise,
Led by some tortuosity of mind,
    Not to believe my verse and their own eyes,
And cry that they 'the moral cannot find,'
    I tell him, if a clergyman, he lies;
Should captains the remark, or critics, make,
They also lie too – under a mistake.

CCIX

The public approbation I expect,
    And beg they'll take my word about the moral,
Which I with their amusement will connect
    (So children cutting teeth receive a coral);
Meantime they'll doubtless please to recollect
    My epical pretensions to the laurel:
For fear some prudish readers should grow skittish,
I've bribed my Grandmother's Review – the British.

CCX

I sent it in a letter to the Editor,
    Who thank'd me duly by return of post –
I'm for a handsome article his creditor;
    Yet, if my gentle Muse he please to roast,
And break a promise after having made it her,
    Denying the receipt of what it cost,
And smear his page with gall instead of honey,
All I can say is – that he had the money.

CCXI

I think that with this holy new alliance
    I may ensure the public, and defy
All other magazines of art or science,
    Daily, or monthly, or three monthly; I
Have not essay'd to multiply their clients,
    Because they tell me 'twere in vain to try,
And that the Edinburgh Review and Quarterly
Treat a dissenting author very martyrly.

CCXII

'*Non ego hoc ferrem calida juventa*
    Consule Planco,' Horace said, and so
Say I; by which quotation there is meant a
    Hint that some six or seven good years ago
(Long ere I dreamt of dating from the Brenta)
    I was most ready to return a blow,
And would not brook at all this sort of thing
In my hot youth – when George the Third was King.

CCXIII

But now at thirty years my hair is grey —
   (I wonder what it will be like at forty?
I thought of a peruke the other day —)
   My heart is not much greener; and, in short, I
Have squander'd my whole summer while 'twas May,
   And feel no more the spirit to retort; I
Have spent my life, both interest and principal,
And deem not, what I deem'd, my soul invincible.

CCXIV

No more — no more — Oh! never more on me
   The freshness of the heart can fall like dew,
Which out of all the lovely things we see
   Extracts emotions beautiful and new;
Hived in our bosoms like the bag o' the bee.
   Think'st thou the honey with those objects grew?
Alas! 'twas not in them, but in thy power
To double even the sweetness of a flower.

CCXV

No more – no more – Oh! never more, my heart,
    Canst thou be my sole world, my universe!
Once all in all, but now a thing apart,
    Thou canst not be my blessing or my curse:
The illusion's gone for ever, and thou art
    Insensible, I trust, but none the worse,
And in thy stead I've got a deal of judgment,
Though heaven knows how it ever found a lodgment.

CCXVI

My days of love are over; me no more
    The charms of maid, wife, and still less of widow,
Can make the fool of which they made before, –
    In short, I must not lead the life I did do;
The credulous hope of mutual minds is o'er,
    The copious use of claret is forbid too,
So for a good old-gentlemanly vice,
I think I must take up with avarice.

CCXVII

Ambition was my idol, which was broken
    Before the shrines of Sorrow, and of Pleasure;
And the two last have left me many a token
    O'er which reflection may be made at leisure;
Now, like Friar Bacon's brazen head, I've spoken,
    'Time is, Time was, Time's past'; – a chymic treasure
Is glittering youth, which I have spent betimes –
My heart in passion, and my head on rhymes.

CCXVIII

What is the end of fame? 'tis but to fill
    A certain portion of uncertain paper:
Some liken it to climbing up a hill,
    Whose summit, like all hills, is lost in vapour;
For this men write, speak, preach, and heroes kill,
    And bards burn what they call their 'midnight taper,'
To have, when the original is dust,
A name, a wretched picture, and worse bust.

CCXIX

What are the hopes of man? Old Egypt's King
 Cheops erected the first pyramid
And largest, thinking it was just the thing
 To keep his memory whole, and mummy hid:
But somebody or other rummaging,
 Burglariously broke his coffin's lid:
Let not a monument give you or me hopes,
Since not a pinch of dust remains of Cheops.

CCXX

But I, being fond of true philosophy,
 Say very often to myself, 'Alas!
All things that have been born were born to die,
 And flesh (which Death mows down to hay) is grass;
You've pass'd your youth not so unpleasantly,
 And if you had it o'er again — 'twould pass —
So thank your stars that matters are no worse,
And read your Bible, sir, and mind your purse.'

CCXXI

But for the present, gentle reader! and
    Still gentler purchaser! the bard – that's I –
Must, with permission, shake you by the hand,
    And so your humble servant, and goodbye!
We meet again, if we should understand
    Each other; and if not, I shall not try
Your patience further than by this short sample –
'Twere well if others follow'd my example.

CCXXII

'Go, little book, from this my solitude!
    I cast thee on the waters – go thy ways!
And if, as I believe, thy vein be good,
    The world will find thee after many days.'
When Southey's read, and Wordsworth understood,
    I can't help putting in my claim to praise –
The four first rhymes are Southey's, every line:
For God's sake, reader! take them not for mine!

From CANTO THE SECOND

Having set sail from Cadiz, Juan is shipwrecked and discovered by Haidée and her maid.

CXV

And lifting him with care into the cave,
    The gentle girl, and her attendant, – one
Young, yet her elder, and of brow less grave,
    And more robust of figure – then begun
To kindle fire, and as the new flames gave
    Light to the rocks that roof'd them, which the sun
Had never seen, the maid, or whatsoe'er
She was, appear'd distinct, and tall, and fair.

CXVI

Her brow was overhung with coins of gold,
    That sparkled o'er the auburn of her hair,
Her clustering hair, whose longer locks were roll'd
    In braids behind; and though her stature were
Even of the highest for a female mould,
    They nearly reach'd her heel; and in her air
There was a something which bespoke command,
As one who was a lady in the land.

CXVII

Her hair, I said, was auburn; but her eyes
    Were black as death, their lashes the same hue,
Of downcast length, in whose silk shadow lies
    Deepest attraction; for when to the view
Forth from its raven fringe the full glance flies,
    Ne'er with such force the swiftest arrow flew;
'Tis as the snake late coil'd, who pours his length,
And hurls at once his venom and his strength.

CXVIII

Her brow was white and low, her cheek's pure dye
    Like twilight rosy still with the set sun;
Short upper lip – sweet lips! that make us sigh
    Ever to have seen such; for she was one
Fit for the model of a statuary
    (A race of mere impostors, when all's done –
I've seen much finer women, ripe and real,
Than all the nonsense of their stone ideal).

CXIX

I'll tell you why I say so, for 'tis just
　　One should not rail without a decent cause:
There was an Irish lady, to whose bust
　　I ne'er saw justice done, and yet she was
A frequent model; and if e'er she must
　　Yield to stern Time and Nature's wrinkling laws,
They will destroy a face which mortal thought
Ne'er compass'd, nor less mortal chisel wrought.

CXX

And such was she, the lady of the cave:
　　Her dress was very different from the Spanish,
Simpler, and yet of colours not so grave;
　　For, as you know, the Spanish women banish
Bright hues when out of doors, and yet, while wave
　　Around them (what I hope will never vanish)
The basquina and the mantilla, they
Seem at the same time mystical and gay.

CXXI

But with our damsel this was not the case:
  Her dress was many-colour'd, finely spun;
Her locks curl'd negligently round her face,
  But through them gold and gems profusely shone:
Her girdle sparkled, and the richest lace
  Flow'd in her veil, and many a precious stone
Flash'd on her little hand; but, what was shocking,
Her small snow feet had slippers, but no stocking.

CXXII

The other female's dress was not unlike,
  But of inferior materials: she
Had not so many ornaments to strike,
  Her hair had silver only, bound to be
Her dowry; and her veil, in form alike,
  Was coarser; and her air, though firm, less free;
Her hair was thicker, but less long; her eyes
As black, but quicker, and of smaller size.

CXXIII

And these two tended him, and cheer'd him both
    With food and raiment, and those soft attentions,
Which are – (as I must own) – of female growth,
    And have ten thousand delicate inventions:
They made a most superior mess of broth,
    A thing which poesy but seldom mentions,
But the best dish that e'er was cook'd since Homer's
Achilles order'd dinner for new comers.

CXXIV

I'll tell you who they were, this female pair,
    Lest they should seem princesses in disguise;
Besides, I hate all mystery, and that air
    Of clap-trap, which your recent poets prize;
And so, in short, the girls they really were
    They shall appear before your curious eyes,
Mistress and maid; the first was only daughter
Of an old man, who lived upon the water.

CXXV

A fisherman he had been in his youth,
    And still a sort of fisherman was he;
But other speculations were, in sooth,
    Added to his connexion with the sea,
Perhaps not so respectable, in truth:
    A little smuggling, and some piracy,
Left him, at last, the sole of many masters
Of an ill-gotten million of piastres.

CXXVI

A fisher, therefore, was he, – though of men,
    Like Peter the Apostle, – and he fish'd
For wandering merchant vessels, now and then,
    And sometimes caught as many as he wish'd;
The cargoes he confiscated, and gain
    He sought in the slave-market too, and dish'd
Full many a morsel for that Turkish trade,
By which, no doubt, a good deal may be made.

CXXVII

He was a Greek, and on his isle had built
    (One of the wild and smaller Cyclades)
A very handsome house from out his guilt,
    And there he lived exceedingly at ease;
Heaven knows what cash he got, or blood he spilt,
    A sad old fellow was he, if you please;
But this I know, it was a spacious building,
Full of barbaric carving, paint, and gilding.

CXXVIII

He had an only daughter, call'd Haidée,
    The greatest heiress of the Eastern Isles;
Besides, so very beautiful was she,
    Her dowry was as nothing to her smiles:
Still in her teens, and like a lovely tree
    She grew to womanhood, and between whiles
Rejected several suitors, just to learn
How to accept a better in his turn.

CXXIX

And walking out upon the beach, below
    The cliff, – towards sunset, on that day she found,
Insensible, – not dead, but nearly so, –
    Don Juan, almost famish'd, and half drown'd;
But being naked, she was shock'd, you know,
    Yet deem'd herself in common pity bound,
As far as in her lay, 'to take him in,
A stranger' dying, with so white a skin.

CXXX

But taking him into her father's house
    Was not exactly the best way to save,
But like conveying to the cat the mouse,
    Or people in a trance into their grave;
Because the good old man had so much 'νους,'
    Unlike the honest Arab thieves so brave,
He would have hospitably cured the stranger
And sold him instantly when out of danger.

CXXXI

And therefore, with her maid, she thought it best
    (A virgin always on her maid relies)
To place him in the cave for present rest:
    And when, at last, he open'd his black eyes,
Their charity increased about their guest;
    And their compassion grew to such a size,
It open'd half the turnpike gates to heaven –
(St. Paul says, 'tis the toll which must be given).

CXXXII

They made a fire, – but such a fire as they
    Upon the moment could contrive with such
Materials as were cast up round the bay, –
    Some broken planks, and oars, that to the touch
Were nearly tinder, since so long they lay,
    A mast was almost crumbled to a crutch;
But, by God's grace, here wrecks were in such plenty,
That there was fuel to have furnish'd twenty.

CXXXIII

He had a bed of furs, and a pelisse,
    For Haidée stripp'd her sables off to make
His couch; and, that he might be more at ease,
    And warm, in case by chance he should awake,
They also gave a petticoat apiece,
    She and her maid, – and promised by daybreak
To pay him a fresh visit, with a dish
For breakfast, of eggs, coffee, bread, and fish.

CXXXIV

And thus they left him to his lone repose:
    Juan slept like a top, or like the dead,
Who sleep at last, perhaps (God only knows),
    Just for the present; and in his lull'd head
Not even a vision of his former woes
    Throbb'd in accursed dreams, which sometimes
        spread
Unwelcome visions of our former years,
Till the eye, cheated, opens thick with tears.

CXXXV

Young Juan slept all dreamless: – but the maid,
  Who smooth'd his pillow, as she left the den
Look'd back upon him, and a moment stayed,
  And turn'd, believing that he call'd again.
He slumber'd; yet she thought, at least she said
  (The heart will slip, even as the tongue and pen),
He had pronounced her name – but she forgot
That at this moment Juan knew it not.

CXXXVI

And pensive to her father's house she went,
  Enjoining silence strict to Zoe, who
Better than her knew what, in fact, she meant,
  She being wiser by a year or two:
A year or two's an age when rightly spent,
  And Zoe spent hers, as most women do,
In gaining all that useful sort of knowledge
Which is acquired in Nature's good old college.

CXXXVII

The morn broke, and found Juan slumbering still
    Fast in his cave, and nothing clash'd upon
His rest: the rushing of the neighbouring rill,
    And the young beams of the excluded sun,
Troubled him not, and he might sleep his fill;
    And need he had of slumber yet, for none
Had suffer'd more – his hardships were comparative
To those related in my grand-dad's 'Narrative.'

CXXXVIII

Not so Haidée: she sadly toss'd and tumbled,
    And started from her sleep, and, turning o'er,
Dream'd of a thousand wrecks, o'er which she
        stumbled,
    And handsome corpses strew'd upon the shore;
And woke her maid so early that she grumbled,
    And call'd her father's old slaves up, who swore
In several oaths – Armenian, Turk, and Greek –
They knew not what to think of such a freak.

CXXXIX

But up she got, and up she made them get,
  With some pretence about the sun, that makes
Sweet skies just when he rises, or is set;
  And 'tis, no doubt, a sight to see when breaks
Bright Phœbus, while the mountains still are wet
  With mist, and every bird with him awakes,
And night is flung off like a mourning suit
Worn for a husband, – or some other brute.

CXL

I say, the sun is a most glorious sight:
  I've seen him rise full oft, indeed of late
I have sat up on purpose all the night,
  Which hastens, as physicians say, one's fate;
And so all ye, who would be in the right
  In health and purse, begin your day to date
From daybreak, and when coffin'd at four-score
Engrave upon the plate, you rose at four.

CXLI

And Haidée met the morning face to face;
   Her own was freshest, though a feverish flush
Had dyed it with the headlong blood, whose race
   From heart to cheek is curb'd into a blush,
Like to a torrent which a mountain's base,
   That overpowers some Alpine river's rush,
Checks to a lake, whose waves in circles spread;
Or the Red Sea — but the sea is not red.

CXLII

And down the cliff the island virgin came,
   And near the cave her quick light footsteps drew,
While the sun smiled on her with his first flame,
   And young Aurora kiss'd her lips with dew,
Taking her for a sister; just the same
   Mistake you would have made on seeing the two,
Although the mortal, quite as fresh and fair,
Had all the advantage, too, of not being air.

CXLIII

And when into the cavern Haidée stepp'd
    All timidly, yet rapidly, she saw
That like an infant Juan sweetly slept;
    And then she stopp'd, and stood as if in awe
(For sleep is awful), and on tiptoe crept
    And wrapt him closer, lest the air, too raw,
Should reach his blood, then o'er him still as death
Bent, with hush'd lips, that drank his scarce-drawn
       breath.

CXLIV

And thus like to an angel o'er the dying
    Who die in righteousness, she lean'd; and there
All tranquilly the shipwreck'd boy was lying,
    As o'er him lay the calm and stirless air:
But Zoe the meantime some eggs was frying,
    Since, after all, no doubt the youthful pair
Must breakfast, and betimes – lest they should ask it,
She drew out her provision from the basket.

CXLV

She knew that the best feelings must have victual,
    And that a shipwreck'd youth would hungry be;
Besides, being less in love, she yawn'd a little,
    And felt her veins chill'd by the neighbouring sea;
And so, she cook'd their breakfast to a tittle;
    I can't say that she gave them any tea,
But there were eggs, fruit, coffee, bread, fish, honey,
With Scio wine, – and all for love, not money.

CXLVI

And Zoe, when the eggs were ready, and
    The coffee made, would fain have waken'd Juan;
But Haidée stopp'd her with her quick small hand,
    And without word, a sign her finger drew on
Her lip, which Zoe needs must understand;
    And, the first breakfast spoilt, prepared a new one,
Because her mistress would not let her break
That sleep which seem'd as it would ne'er awake.

CXLVII

For still he lay, and on his thin worn cheek
    A purple hectic play'd like dying day
On the snow-tops of distant hills; the streak
    Of sufferance yet upon his forehead lay,
Where the blue veins look'd shadowy, shrunk, and
      weak;
    And his black curls were dewy with the spray,
Which weigh'd upon them yet, all damp and salt,
Mix'd with the stony vapours of the vault.

CXLVIII

And she bent o'er him, and he lay beneath,
    Hush'd as the babe upon its mother's breast,
Droop'd as the willow when no winds can breathe,
    Lull'd like the depth of ocean when at rest,
Fair as the crowning rose of the whole wreath,
    Soft as the callow cygnet in its nest;
In short, he was a very pretty fellow,
Although his woes had turn'd him rather yellow.

CXLIX

He woke and gazed, and would have slept again,
  But the fair face which met his eyes forbade
Those eyes to close, though weariness and pain
  Had further sleep a further pleasure made;
For woman's face was never form'd in vain
  For Juan, so that even when he pray'd
He turn'd from grisly saints, and martyrs hairy,
To the sweet portraits of the Virgin Mary.

CL

And thus upon his elbow he arose,
  And look'd upon the lady, in whose cheek
The pale contended with the purple rose,
  As with an effort she began to speak;
Her eyes were eloquent, her words would pose,
  Although she told him, in good modern Greek,
With an Ionian accent, low and sweet,
That he was faint, and must not talk, but eat.

CLI

Now Juan could not understand a word,
　　Being no Grecian; but he had an ear,
And her voice was the warble of a bird,
　　So soft, so sweet, so delicately clear,
That finer, simpler music ne'er was heard;
　　The sort of sound we echo with a tear,
Without knowing why – an overpowering tone,
Whence melody descends as from a throne.

CLII

And Juan gazed as one who is awoke
　　By a distant organ, doubting if he be
Not yet a dreamer, till the spell is broke
　　By the watchman, or some such reality,
Or by one's early valet's cursed knock;
　　At least it is a heavy sound to me,
Who like a morning slumber – for the night
Shows stars and women in a better light.

CLIII

And Juan, too, was help'd out from his dream,
    Or sleep, or whatsoe'er it was, by feeling
A most prodigious appetite; the steam
    Of Zoe's cookery no doubt was stealing
Upon his senses, and the kindling beam
    Of the new fire, which Zoe kept up, kneeling,
To stir her viands, made him quite awake
And long for food, but chiefly a beef-steak.

CLIV

But beef is rare within these oxless isles;
    Goat's flesh there is, no doubt, and kid, and mutton,
And, when a holiday upon them smiles,
    A joint upon their barbarous spits they put on:
But this occurs but seldom, between whiles,
    For some of these are rocks with scarce a hut on;
Others are fair and fertile, among which
This, though not large, was one of the most rich.

CLV

I say that beef is rare, and can't help thinking
    That the old fable of the Minotaur –
From which our modern morals, rightly shrinking,
    Condemn the royal lady's taste who wore
A cow's shape for a mask – was only (sinking
    The allegory) a mere type, no more,
That Pasiphae promoted breeding cattle,
To make the Cretans bloodier in battle.

CLVI

For we all know that English people are
    Fed upon beef – I won't say much of beer,
Because 'tis liquor only, and being far
    From this my subject, has no business here;
We know, too, they are very fond of war,
    A pleasure – like all pleasures – rather dear;
So were the Cretans – from which I infer
That beef and battles both were owing to her.

CLVII

But to resume. The languid Juan raised
　　His head upon his elbow, and he saw
A sight on which he had not lately gazed,
　　As all his latter meals had been quite raw,
Three or four things, for which the Lord he praised,
　　And, feeling still the famish'd vulture gnaw,
He fell upon whate'er was offer'd, like
A priest, a shark, an alderman, or pike.

CLVIII

He ate, and he was well supplied; and she,
　　Who watch'd him like a mother, would have fed
Him past all bounds, because she smiled to see
　　Such appetite in one she had deem'd dead:
But Zoe, being older than Haidée,
　　Knew (by tradition, for she ne'er had read)
That famish'd people must be slowly nurst,
And fed by spoonfuls, else they always burst.

CLIX

And so she took the liberty to state,
    Rather by deeds than words, because the case
Was urgent, that the gentleman, whose fate
    Had made her mistress quit her bed to trace
The sea-shore at this hour, must leave his plate,
    Unless he wish'd to die upon the place –
She snatch'd it, and refused another morsel,
Saying, he had gorged enough to make a horse ill.

CLX

Next they – he being naked, save a tatter'd
    Pair of scarce decent trowsers – went to work,
And in the fire his recent rags they scatter'd,
    And dress'd him, for the present, like a Turk,
Or Greek – that is, although it not much matter'd,
    Omitting turban, slippers, pistols, dirk, –
They furnish'd him, entire, except some stitches,
With a clean shirt, and very spacious breeches.

CLXIX

And every morn his colour freshlier came,
  And every day help'd on his convalescence;
'Twas well, because health in the human frame
  Is pleasant, besides being true love's essence,
For health and idleness to passion's flame
  Are oil and gunpowder; and some good lessons
Are also learnt from Ceres and from Bacchus,
Without whom Venus will not long attack us.

CLXX

While Venus fills the heart (without heart really
  Love, though good always, is not quite so good),
Ceres presents a plate of vermicelli, —
  For love must be sustain'd like flesh and blood,
While Bacchus pours out wine, or hands a jelly:
  Eggs, oysters, too, are amatory food;
But who is their purveyor from above
Heaven knows, — it may be Neptune, Pan, or Jove.

CLXXI

When Juan woke he found some good things ready,
    A bath, a breakfast, and the finest eyes
That ever made a youthful heart less steady,
    Besides her maid's, as pretty for their size;
But I have spoken of all this already –
    And repetition's tiresome and unwise, –
Well – Juan, after bathing in the sea,
Came always back to coffee and Haidée.

CLXXII

Both were so young, and one so innocent,
    That bathing pass'd for nothing: Juan seem'd
To her, as 'twere, the kind of being sent,
    Of whom these two years she had nightly dream'd,
A something to be loved, a creature meant
    To be her happiness, and whom she deem'd
To render happy: all who joy would win
Must share it, – Happiness was born a twin.

CLXXIII

It was such pleasure to behold him, such
    Enlargement of existence to partake
Nature with him, to thrill beneath his touch,
    To watch him slumbering, and to see him wake;
To live with him for ever were too much;
    But then the thought of parting made her quake:
He was her own, her ocean-treasure, cast
Like a rich wreck — her first love, and her last.

CLXXIV

And thus a moon roll'd on, and fair Haidée
    Paid daily visits to her boy, and took
Such plentiful precautions, that still he
    Remain'd unknown within his craggy nook;
At last her father's prows put out to sea,
    For certain merchantmen upon the look,
Not as of yore to carry off an Io,
But three Ragusan vessels bound for Scio.

CLXXV

Then came her freedom, for she had no mother,
  So that, her father being at sea, she was
Free as a married woman, or such other
  Female, as where she likes may freely pass,
Without even the encumbrance of a brother,
  The freest she that ever gazed on glass:
I speak of Christian lands in this comparison,
Where wives, at least, are seldom kept in garrison.

CLXXVI

Now she prolong'd her visits and her talk
  (For they must talk), and he had learnt to say
So much as to propose to take a walk, –
  For little had he wander'd since the day
On which, like a young flower snapp'd from the stalk,
  Drooping and dewy on the beach he lay, –
And thus they walk'd out in the afternoon,
And saw the sun set opposite the moon.

CLXXVII

It was a wild and breaker-beaten coast,
  With cliffs above, and a broad sandy shore,
Guarded by shoals and rocks as by an host,
  With here and there a creek, whose aspect wore
A better welcome to the tempest-tost;
  And rarely ceased the haughty billow's roar,
Save on the dead long summer days, which make
The outstretch'd ocean glitter like a lake.

CLXXVIII

And the small ripple spilt upon the beach
  Scarcely o'erpass'd the cream of your champagne.
When o'er the brim the sparkling bumpers reach,
  That spring-dew of the spirit! the heart's rain!
Few things surpass old wine; and they may preach
  Who please, – the more because they preach in vain, –
Let us have wine and women, mirth and laughter,
Sermons and soda-water the day after.

CLXXIX

Man, being reasonable, must get drunk;
  The best of life is but intoxication:
Glory, the grape, love, gold, in these are sunk
  The hopes of all men, and of every nation;
Without their sap, how branchless were the trunk
  Of life's strange tree, so fruitful on occasion!
But to return, – Get very drunk; and when
You wake with headache, you shall see what then.

CLXXX

Ring for your valet – bid him quickly bring
  Some hock and soda-water, then you'll know
A pleasure worthy Xerxes the great king;
  For not the blest sherbet, sublimed with snow,
Nor the first sparkle of the desert spring,
  Nor Burgundy in all its sunset glow,
After long travel, ennui, love, or slaughter,
Vie with that draught of hock and soda-water.

CLXXXI

The coast – I think it was the coast that I
   Was just describing – Yes, it *was* the coast –
Lay at this period quiet as the sky,
   The sands untumbled, the blue waves untost,
And all was stillness, save the sea-bird's cry,
   And dolphin's leap, and little billow crost
By some low rock or shelve, that made it fret
Against the boundary it scarcely wet.

CLXXXII

And forth they wander'd, her sire being gone,
   As I have said, upon an expedition;
And mother, brother, guardian, she had none,
   Save Zoe, who, although with due precision
She waited on her lady with the sun,
   Thought daily service was her only mission,
Bringing warm water, wreathing her long tresses,
And asking now and then for cast-off dresses.

CLXXXIII

It was the cooling hour, just when the rounded
    Red sun sinks down behind the azure hill,
Which then seems as if the whole earth it bounded,
    Circling all nature, hush'd, and dim, and still,
With the far mountain-crescent half surrounded
    On one side, and the deep sea calm and chill,
Upon the other, and the rosy sky,
With one star sparkling through it like an eye.

CLXXXIV

And thus they wander'd forth, and hand in hand,
    Over the shining pebbles and the shells,
Glided along the smooth and harden'd sand,
    And in the worn and wild receptacles
Work'd by the storms, yet work'd as it were plann'd,
    In hollow halls, with sparry roofs and cells,
They turn'd to rest; and, each clasp'd by an arm,
Yielded to the deep twilight's purple charm.

CLXXXV

They look'd up to the sky, whose floating glow
    Spread like a rosy ocean, vast and bright;
They gazed upon the glittering sea below,
    Whence the broad moon rose circling into sight;
They heard the waves splash, and the wind so low,
    And saw each other's dark eyes darting light
Into each other – and, beholding this,
Their lips drew near, and clung into a kiss;

CLXXXVI

A long, long kiss, a kiss of youth, and love,
    And beauty, all concentrating like rays
Into one focus, kindled from above;
    Such kisses as belong to early days,
Where heart, and soul, and sense, in concert move,
    And the blood's lava, and the pulse a blaze,
Each kiss a heart-quake, – for a kiss's strength,
I think it must be reckon'd by its length.

CLXXXVII

By length I mean duration; theirs endured
    Heaven knows how long – no doubt they never
        reckon'd;
And if they had, they could not have secured
    The sum of their senstions to a second:
They had not spoken; but they felt allured,
    As if their souls and lips each other beckon'd,
Which, being join'd, like swarming bees they clung –
Their hearts the flowers from whence the honey
        sprung.

CLXXXVIII

They were alone, but not alone as they
    Who shut in chambers think it loneliness;
The silent ocean, and the starlight bay,
    The twilight glow, which momently grew less,
The voiceless sands, and dropping caves, that lay
    Around them, made them to each other press,
As if there were no life beneath the sky
Save theirs, and that their life could never die.

CLXXXIX

They fear'd no eyes nor ears on that lone beach,
  They felt no terrors from the night; they were
All in all to each other; though their speech
  Was broken words, they *thought* a language there, –
And all the burning tongues the passions teach
  Found in one sigh the best interpreter
Of nature's oracle – first love, – that all
Which Eve has left her daughters since her fall.

CXC

Haidée spoke not of scruples, ask'd no vows,
  Nor offer'd any; she had never heard
Of plight and promises to be a spouse,
  Or perils by a loving maid incurr'd;
She was all which pure ignorance allows,
  And flew to her young mate like a young bird,
And never having dreamt of falsehood, she
Had not one word to say of constancy.

CXCI

She loved, and was beloved – she adored,
    And she was worshipp'd; after nature's fashion,
Their intense souls, into each other pour'd,
    If souls could die, had perish'd in that passion, –
But by degrees their senses were restored,
    Again to be o'ercome, again to dash on;
And, beating 'gainst *his* bosom, Haidée's heart
Felt as if never more to beat apart.

CXCII

Alas! they were so young, so beautiful,
    So lonely, loving, helpless, and the hour
Was that in which the heart is always full,
    And, having o'er itself no further power,
Prompts deeds eternity cannot annul,
    But pays off moments in an endless shower
Of hell-fire – all prepared for people giving
Pleasure or pain to one another living.

CXCIII

Alas! for Juan and Haidée! they were
  So loving and so lovely – till then never,
Excepting our first parents, such a pair
  Had run the risk of being damn'd for ever;
And Haidée, being devout as well as fair,
  Had, doubtless, heard about the Stygian river,
And hell and purgatory – but forgot
Just in the very crisis she should not.

CXCIV

They look upon each other, and their eyes
  Gleam in the moonlight; and her white arm clasps
Round Juan's head, and his around her lies
  Half buried in the tresses which it grasps:
She sits upon his knee, and drinks his sighs,
  He hers, until they end in broken gasps;
And thus they form a group that's quite antique,
Half naked, loving, natural, and Greek.

CXCV

And when those deep and burning moments pass'd,
    And Juan sunk to sleep within her arms,
She slept not, but all tenderly, though fast,
    Sustain'd his head upon her bosom's charms;
And now and then her eye to heaven is cast,
    And then on the pale cheek her breast now warms,
Pillow'd on her o'erflowing heart, which pants
With all it granted, and with all it grants.

CXCVI

An infant when it gazes on a light,
    A child the moment when it drains the breast,
A devotee when soars the Host in sight,
    An Arab with a stranger for a guest,
A sailor when the prize has struck in fight,
    A miser filling his most hoarded chest,
Feel rapture; but not such true joy are reaping
As they who watch o'er what they love while sleeping.

CXCVII

For there it lies so tranquil, so beloved,
  All that it hath of life with us is living;
So gentle, stirless, helpless, and unmoved,
  And all unconscious of the joy 'tis giving;
All it hath felt, inflicted, pass'd, and proved,
  Hush'd into depths beyond the watcher's diving;
There lies the thing we love with all its errors
And all its charms, like death without its terrors.

CXCVIII

The lady watch'd her lover — and that hour
  Of Love's, and Night's, and Ocean's solitude,
O'erflow'd her soul with their united power;
  Amidst the barren sand and rocks so rude
She and her wave-worn love had made their bower,
  Where nought upon their passion could intrude,
And all the stars that crowded the blue space
Saw nothing happier than her glowing face.

CXCIX

Alas! the love of women! it is known
  To be a lovely and a fearful thing;
For all of theirs upon that die is thrown,
  And if 'tis lost, life hath no more to bring
To them but mockeries of the past alone,
  And their revenge is as the tiger's spring,
Deadly, and quick, and crushing; yet, as real
Torture is theirs, what they inflict they feel.

CC

They are right; for man, to man so oft unjust,
  Is always so to women; one sole bond
Awaits them, treachery is all their trust;
  Taught to conceal, their bursting hearts despond
Over their idol, till some wealthier lust
  Buys them in marriage – and what rests beyond?
A thankless husband, next a faithless lover,
Then dressing, nursing, praying, and all's over.

CCI

Some take a lover, some take drams or prayers,
　　Some mind their household, others dissipation,
Some run away, and but exchange their cares,
　　Losing the advantage of a virtuous station;
Few changes e'er can better their affairs,
　　Theirs being an unnatural situation,
From the dull palace to the dirty hovel:
Some play the devil, and then write a novel.

CCII

Haidée was Nature's bride, and knew not this:
　　Haidée was Passion's child, born where the sun
Showers triple light, and scorches even the kiss
　　Of his gazelle-eyed daughters; she was one
Made but to love, to feel that she was his
　　Who was her chosen: what was said or done
Elsewhere was nothing. She had nought to fear,
Hope, care, nor love beyond, – her heart beat *here*.

CCIII

And oh! that quickening of the heart, that beat!
  How much it costs us! yet each rising throb
Is in its cause as its effect so sweet,
  That Wisdom, ever on the watch to rob
Joy of its alchemy, and to repeat
  Fine truths; even Conscience, too, has a tough job
To make us understand each good old maxim,
So good — I wonder Castlereagh don't tax 'em.

CCIV

And now 'twas done — on the lone shore were plighted
  Their hearts; the stars, their nuptial torches, shed
Beauty upon the beautiful they lighted:
  Oceans their witness, and the cave their bed,
By their own feelings hallow'd and united,
  Their priest was Solitude, and they were wed:
And they were happy, for to their young eyes
Each was an angel, and earth paradise.

CCV

Oh, Love! of whom great Cæsar was the suitor,
   Titus the master, Antony the slave,
Horace, Catullus, scholars, Ovid tutor,
   Sappho the sage blue-stocking, in whose grave
All those may leap who rather would be neuter –
   (Leucadia's rock still overlooks the wave) –
Oh, Love! thou art the very god of evil,
For, after all, we cannot call thee devil.

CCVI

Thou mak'st the chaste connubial state precarious,
   And jestest with the brows of mightiest men:
Cæsar and Pompey, Mahomet, Belisarius,
   Have much employ'd the muse of history's pen:
Their lives and fortunes were extremely various,
   Such worthies Time will never see again;
Yet to these four in three things the same luck holds,
They all were heroes, conquerors, and cuckolds.

CCVII

Thou mak'st philosophers; there's Epicurus
    And Aristippus, a material crew!
Who to immoral courses would allure us
    By theories quite practicable too;
If only from the devil they would insure us,
    How pleasant were the maxim (not quite new),
'Eat, drink, and love; what can the rest avail us?'
So said the royal sage Sardanapalus.

CCVIII

But Juan! had he quite forgotten Julia?
    And should he have forgotten her so soon?
I can't but say it seems to me most truly a
    Perplexing question; but, no doubt, the moon
Does these things for us, and whenever newly a
    Strong palpitation rises, 'tis her boon,
Else how the devil is it that fresh features
Have such a charm for us poor human creatures?

CCIX

I hate inconstancy – I loathe, detest,
    Abhor, condemn, abjure the mortal made
Of such quicksilver clay that in his breast
    No permanent foundations can be laid;
Love, constant love, has been my constant guest,
    And yet last night, being at a masquerade,
I saw the prettiest creature, fresh from Milan,
Which gave me some sensations like a villain.

CCX

But soon Philosophy came to my aid,
    And whisper'd, 'Think of every sacred tie!'
'I will, my dear Philosophy!' I said,
    'But then her teeth, and then, oh, Heaven! her eye!
I'll just inquire if she be wife or maid,
    Or neither – out of curiosity.'
'Stop!' cried Philosophy, with air so Grecian
(Though she was masqued then as a fair Venetian);

283

CCXI

'Stop!' so I stopp'd. – But to return: that which
Men call inconstancy is nothing more
Than admiration due where nature's rich
Profusion with young beauty covers o'er
Some favour'd object; and as in the niche
A lovely statue we almost adore,
This sort of adoration of the real
Is but a heightening of the *beau idéal*.

CCXII

'Tis the perception of the beautiful,
A fine extension of the faculties,
Platonic, universal, wonderful,
Drawn from the stars, and filter'd through the skies,
Without which life would be extremely dull;
In short, it is the use of our own eyes,
With one or two small senses added, just
To hint that flesh is form'd of fiery dust.

CCXIII

Yet 'tis a painful feeling, and unwilling,
  For surely if we always could perceive
In the same object graces quite as killing
  As when she rose upon us like an Eve,
'Twould save us many a heart-ache, many a shilling
  (For we must get them any how, or grieve),
Whereas, if one sole lady pleased for ever,
How pleasant for the heart, as well as liver!

CCXIV

The heart is like the sky, a part of heaven,
  But changes night and day, too, like the sky;
Now o'er it clouds and thunder must be driven,
  And darkness and destruction as on high:
But when it hath been scorch'd, and pierced, and riven,
  Its storms expire in water-drops; the eye
Pours forth at last the heart's blood turn'd to tears,
Which make the English climate of our years.

CCXV

The liver is the lazaret of bile,
  But very rarely executes its function,
For the first passion stays there such a while,
  That all the rest creep in and form a junction,
Like knots of vipers on a dunghill's soil,
  Rage, fear, hate, jealousy, revenge, compunction,
So that all mischiefs spring up from this entrail,
Like earthquakes from the hidden fire call'd 'central.'

CCXVI

In the mean time, without proceeding more
  In this anatomy, I've finish'd now
Two hundred and odd stanzas as before,
  That being about the number I'll allow
Each canto of the twelve, or twenty-four;
  And, laying down my pen, I make my bow,
Leaving Don Juan and Haidée to plead
For them and theirs with all who deign to read.

INDEX OF FIRST LINES